How to
Be
the
MAIN
CHARACTER

70+ EXERCISES FOR
SELF-DISCOVERY AND EMPOWERMENT!

How to
Be
the
MAIN
CHARACTER

A WORKBOOK FOR BECOMING
THE STAR OF YOUR OWN STORY

CRYSTAL ST. JOHN

ADAMS MEDIA
NEW YORK LONDON TORONTO SYDNEY NEW DELHI

Adams Media
An Imprint of Simon & Schuster, Inc.
100 Technology Center Drive
Stoughton, Massachusetts 02072

First Adams Media trade paperback edition January 2022

ADAMS MEDIA and colophon are trademarks of Simon & Schuster.

For information about special discounts for bulk purchases, please contact Simon & Schuster Special Sales at 1-866-506-1949 or business@simonandschuster.com.

The Simon & Schuster Speakers Bureau can bring authors to your live event. For more information or to book an event contact the Simon & Schuster Speakers Bureau at 1-866-248-3049 or visit our website at www.simonspeakers.com.

Interior design by Julia Jacintho and Alaya Howard
Interior images © 123RF/Olga Prozorova, Ienchik; by Alaya Howard

Manufactured in the United States of America

1 2021

ISBN 978-1-5072-1748-1

To my own supporting characters
who have cheered me on,
you are the reason
I have come this far.

And, to my new friend
who feels stuck,
I support you and cheer you on.
Everything you desire
begins right here,
inside of you.
It's waiting to be unlocked
and shared with the world.

CONTENTS

Chapter 3: WHAT MOTIVATES ME?.................................52

Chapter 4: HOW DO I RELATE TO OTHERS?.................62

Chapter 5: WHAT OBSTACLES ARE HOLDING
ME BACK? 72

Chapter 6: HOW DOES MY ATTITUDE AFFECT MY GROWTH?

PART TWO:
A QUEST TO DISCOVER WHO I WANT TO BE... 95

Chapter 7: HOW CAN I DREAM UP A NEW STORY?....96

PART THREE:
A QUEST TO BECOME THAT PERSON... 145

- - - - - - - - - - - - - - - - -

Chapter 12: WHAT ATTITUDE WILL HELP ME THRIVE? 146

Chapter 13: WHAT BOUNDARIES WILL GET ME WHERE I NEED TO GO? 156

Chapter 14: WHAT HABITS WILL GET ME WHERE I NEED TO GO? 164

INTRODUCTION

Have you noticed yourself following along with your life's story instead of boldly taking hold of the pen to write it yourself? Can you remember the last time you were actually *excited* about what you were doing? Do you sometimes feel like an extra in the background of your own movie? It's time to make your way front and center, because, believe it or not, *you* are the main character of your story. You are interesting, you are unique, and you are worthy of the leading role in your life. You have something to share that will move the audience, whoever they might be.

But first you have to believe you are capable of being the main character. You need to be ready to step into the spotlight. You need to know what you want to say and where you want this story to go in the future. Not sure where to start? That's okay! You're about to embark on a journey through the more than seventy activities in this book, to discover your best self and how to show off that amazing person—that main character—to the rest of the world through quests of self-awareness, imagination, and creation.

In Part 1, you'll embark on a quest to discover who you are. You'll identify the talents and qualities that make you unique, and gain insights into how your relationships with others play a role in creating the person you show yourself to be. Once you've dug deep into who you are, you'll start exploring who you *want* to be. In Part 2, you'll uncover your unique purpose, build confidence, and consider new possibilities for your ideal future self. Then, in Part 3, you'll take steps to become that person. You'll set the attitude, boundaries, and habits that will take you to where you need to go, and release anything that isn't helpful in achieving your goals.

You don't get dress rehearsals for living life. You can't yell "Cut!" and start a scene over from the top. You step into the moment, in the best way you can. You grow as you go!

So if you're waiting for something in order to start really living, it's time to stop. Stop waiting for a relationship, waiting to be done with school, waiting to find that next job, or waiting to look a certain way. It's time to start romanticizing the everyday moments you're living through right now. Because all you need to be is you.

PUT YOUR ROSE-COLORED GLASSES ON

It's easy to feel overwhelmed by life. It's easy to feel small, to feel indecisive about what to pursue, or to feel stuck worrying about others' opinions or whether or not you'll fail. It's easy to make your life about appearing successful to everyone else, rather than actually feeling successful inside. This, my friend, is an easy trap to fall into, and one you'll want to avoid. Because you were designed to be vibrant. Not like anyone else, but effortlessly like you!

So what's holding you back? The lie is that the grass is greener over "there" where your external circumstances are different. The truth? Your internal narrative is what changes your external circumstances, or at least the way you feel about them. When you put your rose-colored glasses on and begin to see how much possibility and wonder exists right where you are—with what you have—you won't wish you were living someone else's life. Everything you need is inside of you! This is where romanticizing comes in.

WHAT DOES IT MEAN TO ROMANTICIZE YOUR LIFE?

Romanticizing your life means embracing your life with your whole heart. It's knowing your own power and owning the skin you live in. It's self-love that looks like a good skincare routine, and also the confidence to say no to leave room for a bigger yes somewhere else. It's using your imagination to engage the world and make it a better place for others. It's trusting yourself and not taking setbacks or rejections personally. It's knowing you belong—not because someone else invited you, but because you decided you belong to yourself. And that kind of energy is magnetic!

But how do you start romanticizing ordinary things and moments? It starts with awareness. It starts the moment you are present. And when you are aware of this very moment, you see and notice how magical it actually is. For example, ordinary might look like: "The sun is shining through my window." Romantic looks like: "This bright, warm ball of energy in the sky lights up my space, allowing me to see the colors and textures of everything around me. I feel warm, comforted, and hopeful." Ordinary: "There is a plant in the corner of the room." Romantic: "That plant makes this room more vibrant and fresh. I'm grateful I can keep it alive and it can keep me company. Watching it reminds me that growth happens not when I'm waiting around for it but when I'm out living my life."

Exercise:

Write down five things around you that could be seen as "ordinary." Then describe them "romantically."

1.

2.

3.

4.

5.

WHAT DOES IT MEAN TO BE THE MAIN CHARACTER?

Let's talk about being the main character. A main character is a main character because they are interesting, right? But what makes them interesting? And why do we root for them to succeed?

Well, it's important to note that a main character is always on a quest for something that they want. This quest usually plays out in one of two ways: First, there's the story in which the main character seeks something that they *think* will make them happy, only for us to watch them go on a journey to discover it doesn't *actually* fulfill them. Maybe what they wanted was the dream boy, the prestige, or the job that would make their family proud. But eventually they find that they weren't being true to themselves, or that their desire impacted others negatively. Their ego was pushing them forward.

The second kind of story is the one in which the main character wants something that is bigger than themselves—something that will help make the lives of others better. This type of quest is fueled by what we know as the most powerful force in the universe: love. We always want *that* main character to get what they want, whether it's taking a risk to bring about social justice or pursuing the love of their life. These main characters are operating out of their higher self, their true self. They don't need to prove their value: They see where they can add value by giving what they already have.

Exercise:

Consider your favorite movies and books. Of these favorites, identify the two kinds of main characters: those who feel like they are at a deficit and are driven to take whatever they can get, versus those who see beyond their own wants and use what they have to contribute something to the world.

Main Characters Who Want to Give:

Main Characters Who Want to Take:

HOW DO WE DEFINE "MAIN CHARACTER ENERGY"?

Here's the science: Psychology tells us that the very qualities we admire in others are the same qualities that live inside of us. In other words, we notice certain attributes in others because we are projecting what is already inside of us onto that other person.

With some intention and practice, you can bring these inspiring qualities within you out into the open. Consider the qualities you observe in people you admire most. What is it about them you love? Do they light up a room with their charisma? Are they good at striking up a conversation with the local barista? Do they know how to laugh at themselves in a crisis? Do they relentlessly speak their mind? Are they thoughtful, courageous, organized, stylish, or spiritual? Think about the admirable, magnetic energy they bring with them wherever they go, communicating to you that they are living as the main character of their own story.

Exercise:

Think of the people in your life who you believe embody the "Main character" concept. What makes them interesting? What makes them magnetic? Write down those qualities here.

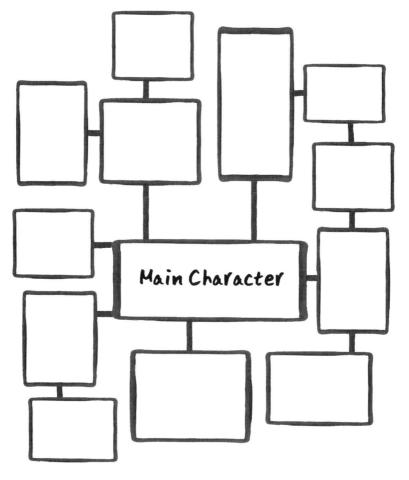

PART ONE

A Quest to Discover Who I Am

In order to be the main character of your life and the story you're writing, you must know who you are. You must become self-aware. Self-awareness will be your guide to help you discover your purpose and your path. If you feel stuck or small, I can promise you it's only because you don't fully see who you are and what you're capable of just yet! The story of your life will include unfolding all of that.

But you have to choose yourself for this story. Self-awareness, and love for that self—you—starts with taking an honest look in the mirror. It involves noticing and admiring the good qualities, accepting the challenging ones, and recognizing that you are no less than the people you admire most. You are full of potential. You are an interesting human—so don't be selfish and hide it. You stand out in your own way when you fully embrace and learn how to effortlessly be the youest you. Let's get to know you, main character!

CHAPTER 1

What Am I Good At?

As we dive into discovering who you are, let's start with some innate qualities about you. What are you naturally good at? What makes you feel powerful when you do it because it is hardwired into your biology? Maybe you know exactly what you're good at. Or maybe you're struggling to feel like you're truly good at anything. (I can promise you, you are good at things!)

A quote often attributed to Albert Einstein says, "Everybody is a genius, but if you judge a fish by its ability to climb a tree, it will live its whole life believing it is stupid." Maybe it seems like everyone else is climbing trees, so you should be too, but it's time to embrace the fact that you have your own unique strengths. So, let's dive in and focus on *your* genius. First, we'll start with what you already know to be true about yourself. As you work through these exercises, let yourself think outside the box. Don't worry about what you think your answers "should" be. The more honest and specific you can be with yourself, the better.

EXPLORING HANDS-ON TALENTS:
THE SUPERPOWERS I CAN SEE

You have what we will call superpowers that are unique to only you. These physical abilities and strengths make you an original.

Often we think of superpowers as exotic abilities in an imagined fantasy world, like being able to fly or walk through walls. And while these powers would be awesome, in real life you have your own hands-on talents that are practically exotic to others who don't share those same strengths. It can be easy to see abilities in others that look different than our own and feel like we are missing out, but that just takes away from realizing and using our own powers. Imagine if Batman just walked around feeling sorry for himself because he didn't have the same natural ability to fly as Superman. He wouldn't be the Batman we love.

Even if you sometimes seem dull to yourself, no one else is an exact replica of you and all your abilities. And this uniqueness is your greatest strength. All of these abilities add up to the one and only you. For example, maybe you can project your voice really well, are really good at running long distances, have a friendly demeanor that makes you approachable, or have a smile that lights up a room.

Exercise:

Identify your physical strengths. What makes you physically unique? What comes easy for you physically? Write down the positive attributes that describe you physically. What can people see and admire about you?

My Physical Strengths:

1.

2.

3.

4.

5.

EXPLORING INTERNAL QUALITIES:
THE SUPERPOWERS I CAN FEEL

You identified your physical strengths that are biologically hardwired into you, but there is so much more to you than that! There are strengths that can't be seen in the same way that make you a force to be reckoned with. These are your internal strengths. Likely, these strengths have been built up through your life experience and the influence of your environment. These strengths may not be as obvious to you, but they distinguish how you tend to navigate through life.

You could be a super empathetic person because you have been through a lot, so you understand what a lot of situations feel like. You could be extremely dependable because your parents counted on you. You could be very organized because you've lived through a lot of clutter. Think about your experiences and what internal strengths you have gained from your life so far. Maybe you have developed certain qualities out of experiencing a deficit of them, while other qualities you carry because that's what was modeled for you. Identify your internal strengths related to how you think (your mind) and how you relate to others (your heart). For example, in terms of your mind, maybe you are extremely organized and realistic. You do what you say you will do. In terms of your heart, maybe you are patient with others. You keep people's secrets, encourage your friends, and freely give compliments.

Exercise:

Identify what your internal strengths are. What are your positive mental attributes? What are your strengths relationally toward others? Write down your strengths related to your mind in the picture of the brain, and your emotional and relational strengths in the heart.

EXPLORING EXTERNAL CUES:
THINGS I HAVE BEEN COMPLIMENTED ON

There can be a lot to learn from the compliments you get from others. They show exactly what you have that others find value in. They make it clear what kind of influence you have on the people around you just by existing.

Have you ever complimented someone and they reject your compliment because they feel completely different about themselves? It hurts when you see good in someone and discover they can't see it for themself. It can also make you wonder, "Where do others see good in me that I don't see in myself?" Sometimes our self-perception can be a little distorted by our own opinions and the story we continually tell ourself about who we are.

What is it like to be around you and interact with you? How do you make others feel? Compliments are a feedback mechanism that can be your clues. Is there something you get complimented for so often you shrug it off? Perhaps because you don't feel deserving of the compliment or it doesn't match the narrative you tell yourself? Take a moment to think back on these compliments. For example, maybe people have told you that you are really funny, your presence helps them feel at ease, you have a great sense of taste, you are easy to talk to, you are well-versed in pop culture, or you have a great memory.

Exercise:

Fill in the magnifying glasses that follow with the "clues" (a.k.a. compliments) you have gotten from others.

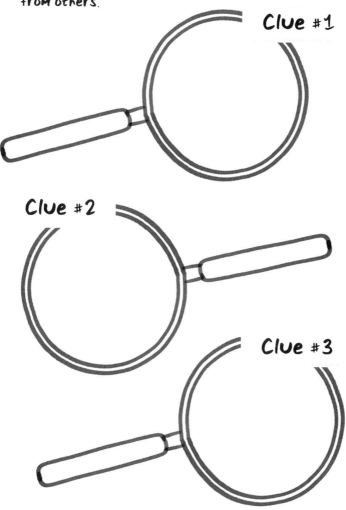

Clue #1

Clue #2

Clue #3

DISCOVERING WHAT MAKES YOU DIFFERENT: MY WEAKNESS IS ACTUALLY MY STRENGTH

What if the very quality about you that makes you feel like you're too much or not enough is actually your most powerful quality? You look different. You act different. You think different. Maybe there's something in your life that you have been teased about or an attribute you felt odd for having. Whatever it is, instead of asking yourself, "What's wrong with me?" try asking, "How can I use this to my advantage?"

Were you the kid who questioned authority? Did you constantly get in trouble for being "too loud"? Or were you so quiet that "shy" is a label you're all too familiar with? Are you stubborn when things don't go your way? Are you super particular about what you like and known as being "high maintenance"? What feels like a weakness is attached to a strength. If you're stubborn, you're also determined. If you're sensitive, you're also compassionate. It just depends on how you choose to look at it and use it!

Exercise:

Put on your rose-colored glasses to see how a perceived "weakness" could actually create opportunity for you. How does this quality help you stand out like a pop of color in a black-and-white film? Use new words to rewrite your narrative of weakness into a story of strength using the boxes provided.

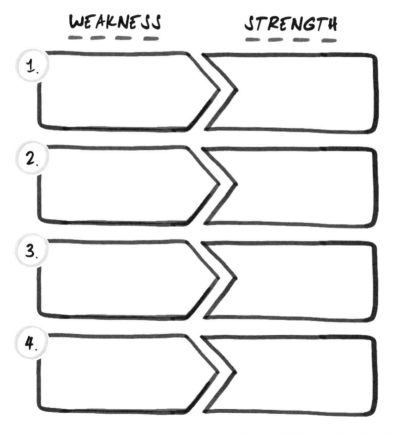

WEAKNESS   STRENGTH

1.

2.

3.

4.

IDENTIFYING AFFIRMATIONS
FROM THOSE YOU TRUST:
TRY ON A NEW NARRATIVE

You can learn so much about yourself from a best friend, partner, mentor, parent—you name it. But unless you ask, you might not get the opportunity to find out just what they would say to describe you!

Consider the people in your life who keep you in check. The people who remind you who you are when life gets confusing and heavy to carry. Whose opinions do you value? Who knows you well and has your best interest in mind? These are your supporting characters. A main character always has supporting characters to give them some perspective when they need it most. They also have supporting characters to call out the good they see in them. (You are a supporting character in other people's stories too, but more on that later!)

Exercise:

Identify three supporting characters in your life who truly have your best interest in mind. Ask them: "What do you think is my best quality?" Write down what stands out to you.

Character:

My Best Quality?:

Character:

My Best Quality?:

Character:

My Best Quality?:

CHAPTER 2

When Do I Feel Most Alive?

It's one thing to be naturally gifted with certain abilities; it's a whole other thing to find joy in the everyday practice of these abilities. When you identify the things that you have a natural talent for *and* enjoy doing, that's a hint that you have found a passion.

It can be easy to become distracted by romanticizing results that may look shiny: a masterful art piece, a beautifully produced song, a thriving business, a huge following, a paycheck... But what does the journey to these achievements feel like? Are you actually enjoying it? You may love the idea of how it would feel to meet some external standard for success. But discovering what you love doing every day as a lifestyle—what you are passionate about—is what gives you the patience, grit, and motivation to go far. It's time to get clear on what is *worth* pursuing by identifying what you *enjoy* doing.

DISCOVERING SELF-EXPRESSION:
I LIKE TO EXPRESS MYSELF BY...

Have you ever taken the time to consider all the random things you like doing? How do you love to express yourself? Not just the most obvious things but also the little details of life. Maybe things you would overlook about day-to-day life that genuinely bring you pleasure. Here you will create a collection of everything you love doing, big and small—all the things that make you feel alive.

Do you like telling jokes, making the coffee in the morning, decorating your space, experimenting in the kitchen, planning the vacation itinerary, or sending out holiday cards? Walk yourself through your daily routine. What are your favorite moments of the day? What are you doing in those moments? Consider all the little things that you embrace to show off your desires, point of view, and preferences. These are the ways that you naturally take ownership to express who you are to the world!

Exercise:

Identify the most obvious and important things that you love to do. Fill in those answers on the building blocks that follow, starting with the foundational blocks at the bottom. As you identify other favorites, build onto the building blocks with these more unexpected or unique answers that you might not have considered before.

DISCOVERING WHAT
COMES NATURALLY:
IT FEELS EFFORTLESS WHEN I...

In Chapter 1, you thought about the compliments you've received. Some compliments you may have shrugged off because you didn't feel like you *earned* them. You were being effortlessly yourself, and that felt undeserving of a compliment. Sometimes when something seems easy and natural, you can feel like a fraud when you're praised for it. "I don't deserve that! I didn't have to work for that. What about the things I work really hard for?" And yet, because you didn't have to work hard for it—it flowed effortlessly from your essence—it is exactly the kind of advantage you have that is worth utilizing and building off of!

Imagine seeing yourself from a distance sitting in a café. Or at work. Or out with some friends. What would you notice about yourself? How would you describe your essence—your energy? How do you appear different from others? Similar to others? What is so you it's almost as natural as breathing?

Exercise:

Use your imagination to observe yourself as a stranger would. Focus on the positive qualities you see. Take note of attributes that tempt you to not be kind toward yourself. (More on this later!) Write down what you see.

DISCOVERING HOW
YOU CAN HELP:
I FEEL LIKE I BRING VALUE
TO OTHERS WHEN I...

There are certain roles that you naturally fall into. Why? Because you're good at them. You trust your ability to do the job, and you feel useful as others benefit from your input. So what is a role you usually play?

Say you're at school or work, and there is a group project: What tasks do you lean toward doing? Or imagine you're in a discussion with a group of friends: How do you bring value to the conversation? What about when you're with your family: How do they benefit because you are there? And in your close friendships or relationships, how do others benefit because you are their significant other or friend? Maybe you've even been given nicknames for the roles you tend to play, like being called "mom" by your friends because of how you look after everyone else.

Exercise:

Identify your roles and fill out your name tag. Be creative. It can be whatever you want it to be. List all the ways you enhance others' lives.

IDENTIFYING WHERE YOU SPEND YOUR TIME:
I LOSE TRACK OF TIME WHEN I...

A great way to determine if you enjoy something is whether you lose track of time while you're doing it. Why? Because that means you're being *present*, which is the best place to be at all times. Remember that is what it means to romanticize your life: to be fully present. You create your future by being fully mindful in each moment.

Think about your day today. Did you forget to check your phone while you were doing something? What are the activities that when you're doing them you stop thinking about the future, stop ruminating over the past, and are *fully* where you are? (It's okay if it's something as simple as shopping, watching *Netflix*, or another guilty pleasure.) Acknowledge all your habits—whether they are productive or not! This is about creating all-around self-awareness, which will help you in the quests ahead.

Exercise:

List out all the productive things you lose track of time while doing in the left-hand box, and acknowledge the unproductive or bad habits in the right-hand box.

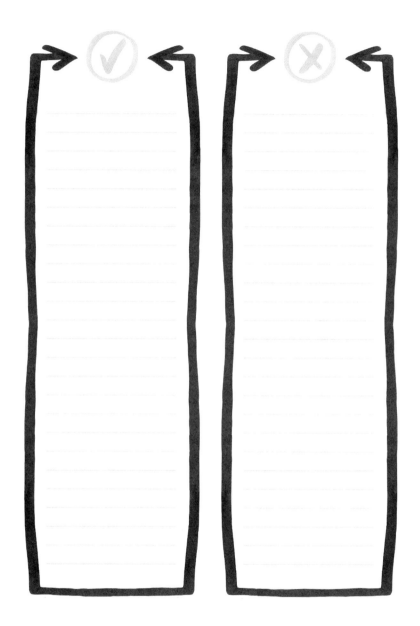

IDENTIFYING WHAT YOU'RE PATIENT WITH:
I HAVE MORE PATIENCE THAN OTHERS WHEN I...

When you enjoy doing something so much that you find the patience within yourself to show up and work at it time and time again, *take note*! Natural talent is all the hype when you're a kid. But as you grow up, you realize talent is not nearly as important as grit. Why? Often, people don't fail at things because they lack talent: They fail because they lack *persistence*. They don't have the determination to see their goals through to the end. Persistence is rare and will set you apart.

What energizes you in such a way that you find the capacity within yourself to keep going when others would have checked out? What subject do you love to talk about way longer than other people do? Is there something you enjoy the meticulous process of working at over and over late into the night? Do you find yourself perpetually curious about a certain topic or practice, and somehow it still hasn't become dull to you?

Maybe something stands out to you immediately, or you might have to think a little deeper to discover your answer. It's okay if you feel like you can't name your passion just yet: You will discover more about yourself as you try more things. In the meantime, work with your current experience. Any answer, no matter how random you think it is, applies!

Exercise:

It's time to investigate. In the magnifying lens, write what sparks your greatest curiosity. List your top enthusiasms that come to mind.

IDENTIFYING WITH YOUR INNER CHILD:
MY EIGHT-YEAR-OLD SELF LOVED...

When you look at the things you were drawn to as a child, you can discover a lot about yourself. What were the passions you had before someone said they weren't "realistic" or you started comparing your abilities to others? Maybe you took interest in things that you weren't the most talented at, or things that wouldn't necessarily have you rolling in the dough as an adult. Regardless, these things provide insight into what you value and what makes you feel alive. And you can creatively shape those passions into the path you're paving.

Maybe you wanted to be a popstar or famous songwriter. True, you can't control whether your voice or a song you wrote will get so much attention you'll become famous for it. But you *can* control whether you take the time to make that music you feel passionate about and find ways to share it. You can control if you let music be a part of your life in some shape or form. Or maybe you wanted to be the president. You can't control all the variables needed to win a presidential election, but you *can* control your active interest in government and politics and how you use your voice to pursue change. When you focus on what you *can* control, doors will open.

Exercise:

What did you desire doing before a person or experience told you it was an impractical dream? Fill in the bubbles with your answers.

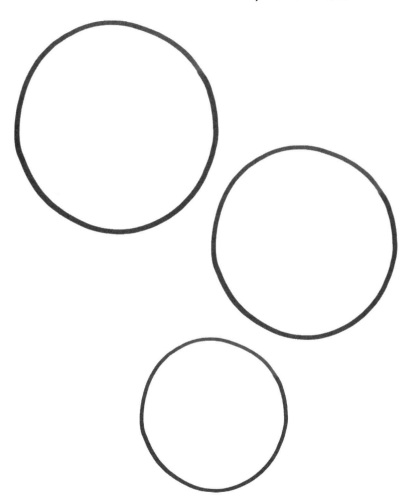

IDENTIFYING WHAT YOU VALUE:
THE COMMON DENOMINATOR IS...

If you look closely at all the things you love and enjoy doing, you can often find an invisible string that runs through all of your passions, like a common denominator. This reveals what you deeply value.

Maybe beauty is what you value. The visual arts captivate you. You find yourself drawn to fashion or interior design, or perhaps you love snapping that perfect picture for your social media. Maybe you value courage. You're up for anything that is going to get you out of your comfort zone and help you grow, be it skydiving, public speaking, or even being vulnerable about your feelings. Maybe you value adventure. You get bored easily and resent anything mundane; you like to travel, pick up unusual hobbies, and meet new people.

Exercise:

When you think about all of the things you love, try to determine what they have in common. Start by writing your passions in the smaller circles. Then, in the larger circles, name the value that these passions share.

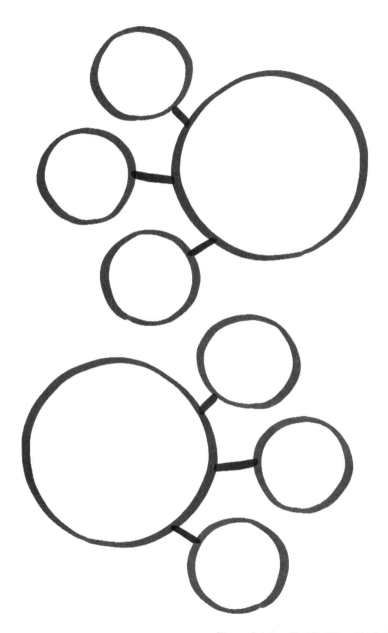

CHAPTER 3

What Motivates Me?

What motivates you? What drives you to keep going, even if things get tough? This is a foundational piece of your life puzzle that, once figured out, will not only compel you to make something of your talents and passions, but also create direction and clarity as to what your unique story is. A lot of other people may be doctors, lawyers, artists, writers, entrepreneurs, etc., but what differentiates you is your "why"—your reason for being a doctor, lawyer, artist, writer, entrepreneur, etc.

When you steer your talents and passions to always serve your "why," you won't be so confused by or tempted toward distractions that present themselves as opportunities. It will be easier to pick out what to say yes to and what to say no to. You'll be focused and intentional. You will create confidence in yourself and in your vision, and that will drive your story as the main character.

IDENTIFYING WHAT YOU WANT TO SEE MORE OF:
I AM MOST INSPIRED BY SEEING _____ IN THE WORLD

We all can imagine a perfect world, and that drives us to do what we can to make it a little better than we found it. What does this perfect world look like to *you*? What do you have inside of you that can play a part in bringing more beauty, function, and connection into that world? Consider the values you discovered in the previous exercise. How do the things you value make the world a better place?

Maybe it's people who go out of their way to pick up trash and take care of the environment. Or the way you feel in the thoughtfully designed ambience of your favorite coffee shop. Maybe it's the boss who cares enough to ask about how you are doing in your personal life. Maybe it's community, or family, or love. These are all examples of bringing more connection, beauty, or function into the world.

Do you think the things that inspire you are created by others who are living as the main character of their life? The most compelling things in the world are made by people who decide to own the life they've been given.

Exercise:

What do you value? Considering the examples, identify what you appreciate that you observe others creating or practicing in their life. What helps connect people? What adds more beauty to the world? What creates better function and flow in life? Fill in your answers in the chart here.

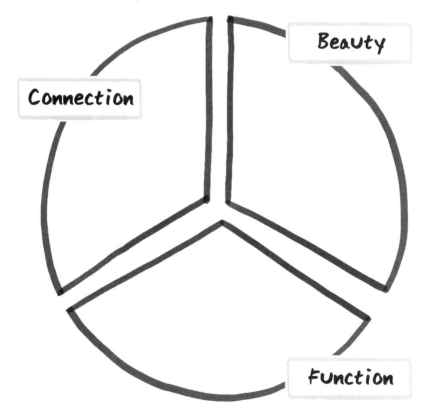

Beauty

Connection

Function

IDENTIFYING WHAT YOU LOOK FORWARD TO:
I AM MOST EXCITED ABOUT THE FUTURE WHEN I THINK OF...

The results you look forward to in your future reveal what motivates you to take action in your life today. But why do you *really* want the things you want? Behind every external achievement you hope for is an expectation that you will finally feel a certain way about yourself and about your life. Discovering what that feeling is that you hope to gain can help you look at things from a different perspective and be honest with yourself. Will achieving actually bring the feeling? Or is achieving a by-product of already creating the feeling inside of yourself?

Will you feel loved when you finally find love? Or will you find love when you finally feel loved? Will you feel like you're enough when you finally receive the award, or will you receive the award because you already discovered that you are enough? Will you feel abundance when you've made the money, or will you make the money because you already feel you're abundant? Be honest with yourself. It's okay to be where you are! Self-awareness will take you to new places.

Exercise:

What excites you just thinking about it coming to life? A relationship, a dream job, being able to support yourself, having a family, your name on an award, or finally getting that degree? List each thing in the first box, and then identify why it makes you feel excited and hopeful in the second box. What will it truly mean for you to have it?

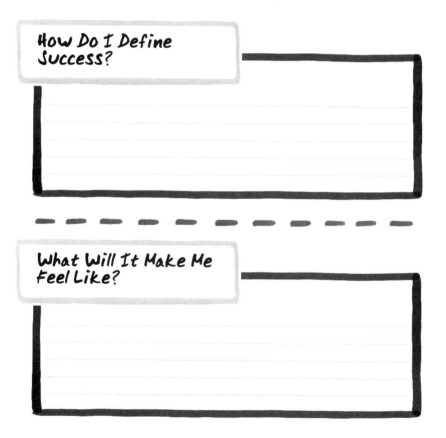

How Do I Define Success?

What Will It Make Me Feel Like?

DISCOVERING YOUR INTENTION:
MY "WHY" IS...

Discovering your "why" often lives within your answer to the question "What breaks my heart?" The things you see around you that make you feel frustrated and angered reveal to you that something is out of alignment: Your values, beliefs, and desires are not being expressed well enough (or they are being violated in some way).

What makes *you* angry? What are you tired of seeing? Has something been unfair or neglected? Whatever you have experienced may have led you spiraling like a tornado; it could have caused pain or limiting beliefs that influence you to this day. But as you begin to heal and discover self-love on your journey of self-awareness, consider how your negative experience could be turned into your cause. How has it given you tools and perspective that you can use to help others?

Instead of running away from feelings of anger and sadness, allow yourself to sit with them. They are trying to tell you something. They are trying to help you see your deepest desires and needs in life. Consider Fred Rogers, the iconic creator of the TV show *Mister Rogers' Neighborhood*. He was bullied as a kid for his weight. He grew up to make a children's program in which he told kids, "I like you just the way you are." He channeled his own painful experience to tell others they didn't need to change anything about themselves to be valued.

Exercise:

Write your cause in the box provided. Fill in the circles with experiences and realizations that inform how you got to this "why."

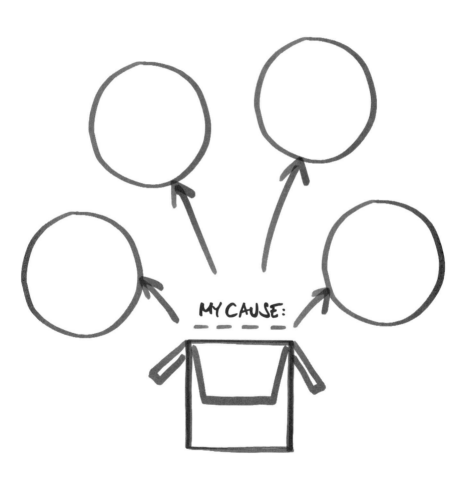

MY CAUSE:

DISCOVERING YOUR PURPOSE:
THREE INGREDIENTS TO CREATE MY PATH ARE...

What do you find when you combine your natural abilities, what you enjoy doing most, and what motivates you (your "why" that you wrote in the previous exercise)? You discover what you want to work toward in life!

Begin to imagine how you can create this unique path. It's not going to look like anyone else's path. As you aspire to show up in the fullness of your personality, life experiences, desires, energy, and all the other things that make up who you are, you will create an original story. You are the pioneer of your own path. Flip back through the pages of Chapter 1 and this chapter, and pick the top choices you came up with in identifying your strengths, what you most enjoy doing, and what motivates you.

Exercise:

Combine the three elements—your strengths, what you enjoy, and your motivations—together here. Begin to imagine how these elements could work together. Write down your ideas in the intersecting areas.

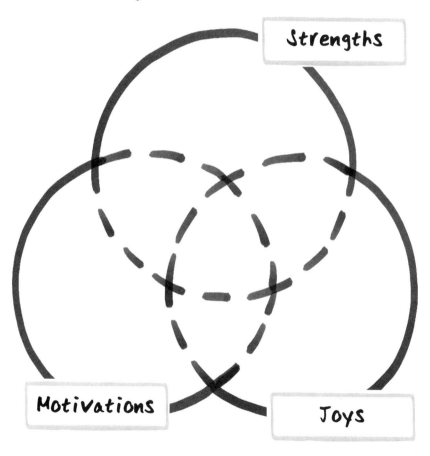

CHAPTER 4

How Do I Relate to Others?

As you discovered your motivation in the previous chapter, you likely became more aware of how others have influenced you in your life. What breaks your heart, what makes you angry, what you desire—these things are not isolated within yourself. You discover them through your relationships with others. Your family, friends, partners, mentors, teachers, even celebrities you admire, are people who speak into your life and shape your way of thinking.

For better or worse, other people have influenced you, and likewise, *you influence others.* Whether that excites you or terrifies you, it's something to be aware of. If you are living and breathing, the choices you make affect other people. So how do you influence others right now? How do you *want* to influence others? And who do you let influence you? As you become the main character, owning and writing your own story, you are definitely going to influence others. And they are going to influence how you live *your* life and write *your* story.

DEFINING INFLUENCE:
HOW DO I SEE INFLUENCE IN OTHERS?

What does it mean to be a person of influence? Consider people in the world who you call "influential." What makes them so special? And how did they get to a place in life where you notice them? Where what they say carries weight? Or the way they dress creates new trends? Why are people inspired by them? Why do people trust them?

Is it because they seem to have connected to this elusive idea of living fully alive, being true to themselves in the things they create? Is it because they dared to go first and make mistakes, or try something with no idea if it would work out? Is it because they have journeyed enough through life to see what really matters, or they have found their identity and are showing up boldly?

No matter who they are, all influential people have at least one thing in common: They took a risk. They bet on themselves. They decided life was worth showing up for. Consider someone like Martin Luther King Jr., who dared to speak his truth, risking his life to inspire others to work for justice. Or music artists like Lady Gaga and Billie Eilish, who have taken bold risks with their fashion choices, distinguishing their identity. Or a serial entrepreneur like Elon Musk, whose high-risk decision-making in building companies and figuring out what companies to invest in has definitely paid off. Apart from not shying away from risk, what else do these influential people share?

Exercise:

Consider influential people you admire and write their names in the small circles. Think about the qualities that these people share. Write these in the larger circle.

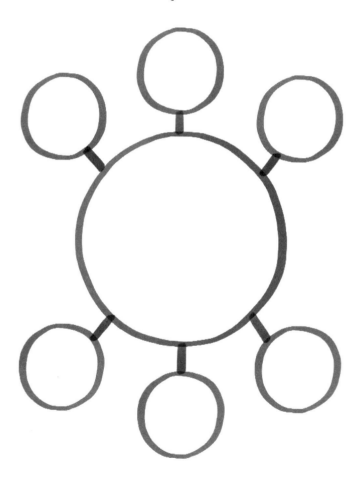

EXAMINING YOUR RELATIONSHIPS:
WHO ARE MY PEOPLE AND HOW DO THEY INFLUENCE ME?

Whether you realize it or not, you are influenced by the people you spend your time with—whether that's your best friends, partner, coworker, or the host of that podcast you listen to all the time. Who do you let have a voice in your life? Whose opinions do you value? Are they living as the main character of their own story? And what do you think of the story they are writing?

The people who you can easily identify as influential arrived at that point because of smaller influences in *their* life. Someone believed in them. Or someone did not believe in them, so they were determined to prove them wrong! The voices in their life pushed them in a direction, shaping their thinking, their choices, and the outcomes you see today. Look around at the people in your own life who have influenced the way you see yourself and the way you see the world. Who are those people? Are they honest with you? Do they give you self-awareness? Constructive feedback? Do you have people who believe in you? Are they taking action in their own life? What motivates them in life? Do they have a good sense of self? Are they navigating life in fear and hesitation or in faith and possibility? Whatever and whoever is in your life—they are going to influence you!

Exercise:

List the ways those closest to you have influenced you in positive ways in the left-hand box. Then take note of negative traits in the people around you and how those have influenced you in the right-hand box.

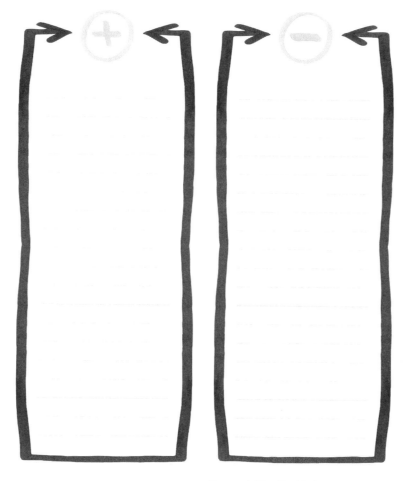

IDENTIFYING YOUR INFLUENCE:
HOW DO I RECOGNIZE MY OWN INFLUENCE?

How do you influence the people closest to you, like friends and family? How do you influence people you interact with daily, like peers, coworkers, clients, and the cashier at the store? In other words, how does who you are and how you show up make a difference in the lives of others?

Just like other people influence you, you influence them too! What do you bring to their story? How do you inspire them and bring positivity and support into their lives? Do you bring any conflict or chaos? Do you hold them back in any way, whether you mean to or not?

Exercise:

Identify ways that you are a positive influence on the five people in your life who you are closest to, and also reflect on ways that you may be negatively influencing them too, whether through gossip, criticism, or a negative attitude. List these influences (write the positive influences in the left-hand box and the negative influences in the right-hand box).

DISCOVERING HOW TO SHARE YOUR INFLUENCE:
HOW DO I WANT TO USE MY INFLUENCE?

Now that you've become more aware of what influence looks like in your life right now, it's time to consider how you *want* it to look. Think about who you want to be in this world. How do you want to relate to others? How do you want others to feel when they interact with you? What impression do you want to leave behind?

You will take more time to imagine in the next quest, so for now focus on how your natural abilities, the things you enjoy doing, your "why," and your unique energy can combine to influence others. How can you use your qualities to write a story that moves your chosen audience?

Exercise:

Refer back to the exercises in the previous chapters. Recall your natural abilities, what makes you feel alive, what motivates you, and your energy. Think about what it is you want to say with your influence.

WHAT I WANT TO SAY:

CHAPTER 5

What Obstacles Are Holding Me Back?

Risk is the path to your deepest desires. It's the key to living fully as the main character! So what fear might be holding you back from taking the leap and discovering all the amazing things that you could write into your story? One main obstacle could be simply the lens through which you're looking at yourself and the world around you. Wherever you feel insecurity about who you are, there are distortions in your lens. You didn't put it there, but you have become quite comfortable with this lens. It's familiar! But if it makes you feel small, incapable, or bad about who you are, it will keep you from confidently stepping into your role as the main character.

When stepping outside of your beliefs, biases, and judgments of how you should be and how others and the world itself should be, you can rewrite the story you tell yourself without all the limiting beliefs and feelings that have kept you feeling small, helpless, and unqualified. It is a gradual process to change your lens, but, through discovering compassion for yourself and others, you can free yourself to write a new story you may have never even dreamt before!

IDENTIFYING YOUR INNER CRITIC:
HOW I JUDGE OTHERS IS HOW I JUDGE MYSELF

In the earlier exercise How Do We Define "Main Character Energy," you identified qualities that you admire in others and learned that those same qualities live somewhere inside of you. There is a flip side to this psychology: Negative qualities that you are quick to notice in others may just be a reflection of your own tendency toward those same qualities. We judge in others what we judge in ourselves. What does this mean? The more criticism you may project onto others, the more criticism you are projecting onto *yourself*. (Oof!)

It might feel good in a moment to judge someone else (and feel like you are better than them in the process), but in the long run it's self-sabotage. You're putting them down *because* you're so critical of yourself. And this inner critic will hold you back from freely embracing your own authentic path. Why? The fear that someone else will criticize *you*! Always worrying about what others think can be so paralyzing that it becomes easier to just play it safe, people-please, and then (sigh) end up resenting others and blaming them for not making it easier for you to write a compelling story! To tame your inner critic, start by becoming aware of it. What do you criticize about how people act, look, or think? And how do you observe these things in yourself?

Exercise:

In the mirror, write negative qualities you tend to notice in others.

IDENTIFYING YOUR SHAME OR LIMITING BELIEFS:
MY NEW INNER DIALOGUE IS...

Now that you've become more aware of your inner critic by observing what you tend to judge in others, it's time to take a deeper look at how that critic may be holding you back. This inner critic is all about shame and insecurities, trying to tell you that you are unworthy and not enough. What does this voice sound like for you?

When you identify what story keeps playing in your head about who you aren't and what disqualifies you, you can start making moves to change this story by suggesting who you *are*. The negative story you've been telling yourself has been repeated so many times that by now it feels like it's who you are, but it's really only a suggestion. *You* get to decide who you are. Override the negative story by suggesting empowering affirmations in its place. Find evidence for what you are affirming so you believe it to be true. For example, if you tell yourself you think too slowly, instead suggest that you are intelligent because you are thoughtful with your words. If you tell yourself no one will love you, suggest that you are lovable because you are a great listener or you make people laugh; you bring value to others just by being yourself! As you practice these affirmations over time, you will feel more and more empowered to show up as the main character.

Exercise:

In the space here, write down what your inner critic tells you, and then flip it around. Turn it into an affirmation that explains why you are good! Additionally, write your answers on sticky notes. Put them on your bedroom mirror or wherever you will see them often. Rewiring your subconscious mind takes repetition! So make it easy to revisit these affirmations.

Inner Critic:
New Suggestion:
because

Inner Critic:
New Suggestion:
because

Inner Critic:
New Suggestion:
because

DEFINING SELF-LOVE:
FORGIVING MYSELF AND FORGIVING OTHERS

You've identified the voice of your inner critic. But where did it come from? You weren't born with it! In order to take full agency of your story, heal from negative past experiences, and step wholeheartedly into your future as the main character, you'll need to get to the root of your limiting beliefs. It's time to think back to the moment a character in your story suggested a critical opinion for the first time, and you accepted it. What if you found that their criticism had nothing to do with you, and everything to do with them projecting their own inner critic onto you? Could it be that they hurt you, because deep down…they were hurting?

Go back to the previous exercise to recall the limiting beliefs you have. Identify when they began. Was it something said, or an impression you got from someone's behavior? Maybe it was the culture of the family you grew up in or a community you have been a part of. Consider how the characters who planted limiting beliefs in you were being weighed down by their own limiting beliefs. Consider how they felt trapped inside of their own inner critic. Criticism is an ongoing cycle that limits everyone. Set yourself free from being defined by someone else's pain. Because their words and behavior are a reflection of the lens they are looking through, not a reflection of you.

Exercise:

What characters in your life have impressed pain or criticism onto you? Try to imagine for a minute what it might have felt like to be in their shoes. Given their own possible experiences, what do you think their inner critic may have sounded like for them at the time? Write compassionately about what might have been affecting them—pushing them to say or do the thing(s) that upset you.

FINDING PRIDE IN WHO YOU ARE: WHAT DO SELF-COMPASSION AND BELONGING LOOK LIKE?

You've identified your inner critic. You've seen how others have influenced you and affected how you see yourself. And you've dared to look at the pain of others through a new lens of compassion. Now you're going to revisit those key moments in your past with compassion for yourself. The obstacles you have faced so far have not disqualified you from being the main character. Actually, they've given your story texture and an interesting plot! When you choose to redefine the challenges you have experienced, you are owning the story and writing it how you want it to be written.

Revisit your past—your inner child—with the information and experience you have today. What does that younger version of you need to hear from present-day you? In choosing to see the past with compassion, what would you say to them? For example, maybe your brother slammed the door in your face, telling you that you weren't invited to a party he was having. Try talking to this younger version of yourself: "You belong. You are welcome. He may have shut the door in your face, but he shut himself out of your party. You are a party! And he doesn't know how to be in the presence of your party."

Exercise:

Insert defining memories from your past in the circles on the following timeline. Now, close your eyes and revisit those moments as your present self. Acknowledge what happened and say what you know now to be the truth over whatever self-critical or not-so-nice assumption you jumped to that day. Use the boxes to write out what your present self has to say about those moments.

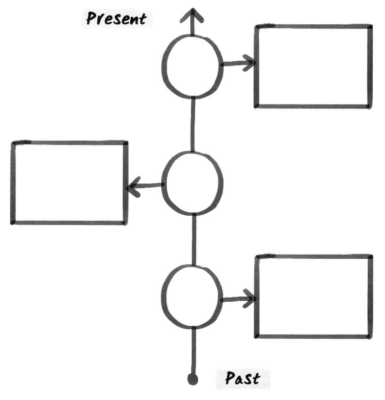

Present

Past

CHAPTER 6

How Does My Attitude Affect My Growth?

The way you see yourself and the world around you affects your attitude and how you show up every day. Earlier, you learned about two different types of main characters. The first character, operating from their ego, sees through a lens of: "I am not enough. I need to convince others of my value!" And the second character, operating from their higher self, sees through a lens of: "I am enough. Now, how can I add value to others?" These characters' circumstances could look identical to yours. But what they make of these situations is completely different because of how they see themselves and how that causes them to see others.

Your attitude is driven by which of these lenses you are looking through. When your ego is running the show, you focus on how things appear. Do you appear successful? Do you appear valuable? Too much concern with how things look and how you compare to others makes it very difficult to show up authentic to who you are and who you are uniquely made to be. However, when you begin to discover your value and lead with your higher self, you are fueled by compassion and abundance, creating the courage you need for risk, vulnerability, and patience to see things through. Seeing your own value helps you relinquish the need to control whether others can see it too.

IDENTIFYING YOUR MOTIVE:
DO I HAVE SOMETHING TO PROVE?

It's important to ask yourself: "Am I trying to prove something?" Being a main character motivated by ego is being a main character who cares more about what everyone else thinks of you than about what *you* think of you. This will make it difficult to build integrity with those around you, but most importantly with yourself! You don't want to find yourself sitting in regret down the road, wondering, "Could this have been better if I'd showed up as myself and not as what I thought everyone else wanted me to be?" As you take the time to become self-aware, discovering your own value, and growing in self-love, you will find it easier to operate from love instead of fear, giving you courage to be authentic and show up fully as your fabulous self.

In Chapter 5, you revisited some defining moments that have hurt your self-image and held you back. Those moments, and other moments, could very well be defining your worldview. Consider: Do you feel like you need to prove something in order to be loved? Do you feel like you need to become something in order to belong? Do you feel like you need to attain something in order to finally be accepted?

We all have egos fractured in different ways. We are all *works in progress*! The important thing is to become aware of where your ego is showing up in your pursuits, desperately trying to take the spotlight (or hide from it to avoid rejection!).

Exercise:

Identify the voice of your ego, then identify the voice of your higher self.

MY HIGHER SELF:

MY EGO:

COUNTERING LIMITING BELIEFS:
IF ONLY I HAD MORE_____,
THEN I COULD THRIVE

Isn't it so easy to live in the future? To attach happiness to getting whatever we don't yet have? "If I had more time, money, resources, connections, energy, etc., *then* I would be fulfilled. *Then* I would take action!" Looking at life this way keeps you from seeing what you *do* have—what is right in front of you waiting for you to make the most of it. The best way to get out of this rut and begin seeing possibility is through practicing gratitude.

You could wait your whole life for all the dots to align, for the scale to finally have the "right" number on it, or for everyone to be on board with your dream. Waiting for the perfect, most convenient moment will leave you waiting for a long time, if not forever! This desire for perfection is driven by your inner critic, worrying what others will think, keeping you from stepping into your dreams and being the main character of your life.

Be honest with yourself: Would you rather risk doing something imperfectly or not do it at all? Consider a time you experienced regret for not trying. Maybe it was a time you wanted to speak up but hesitated, and the moment passed. Or you went with the flow of everyone else, only to leave your authentic self behind. It hurts you when you shrink yourself into playing an extra in your own show! What would happen if you followed your impulse, showed up in your imperfections, and owned that stage?

Exercise:

Identify what you wish you had more control over in your life. For example, "I wish I had more control over how much my job pays me." Then consider what you *do* have control over. For example, "I *do* have control over how I perform at work or coming up with other ways of making money on the side." How can you make the most of it?

I wish I had more control over
but I do have control over ,
.

I wish I had more control over
but I do have control over ,
.

DISCOVERING WHAT'S HOLDING YOU BACK:
I FEEL LIMITED BY...

You are limitless. Well, you are if you *believe* you are. It may seem like there are standards and expectations, and certain things you need to have to qualify for this or that. But the power of what you believe carries the most weight! After all, you don't simply draw into your life what you want and wish for: You draw into your life what you actually believe you're worthy and capable of having. Each belief you carry forms the reality you create and experience every day through your attitude and choices. So what *do* you believe about yourself? About others? About how the world works? Could you be reinforcing limiting beliefs with negative self-talk? For example: "I don't have the personality for that career." "I don't belong with these people." "I'm too old to try this now."

Exercise:

Identify the things you say to yourself that have become facts to you. Consider that maybe they're not true. Maybe you are capable. Maybe you do have it in you. Maybe you are enough. Write down your limiting beliefs in the locks, and rewrite these beliefs into limitless beliefs in or beside the keys.

LEARNING TO TAKE AGENCY OVER YOUR STORY:
THIS HAPPENED ~~TO~~ FOR ME

What if the challenges you face aren't to your disadvantage? What if they are there to help you discover the strength inside of you? What if they are there to teach you something and better prepare you for your wildest dreams? As you start looking at the experiences that have taught you that unfair things happen in life, you can see how your challenges give your story depth. What if your story and strength can inspire others to find their own strength? You can allow what has happened in your story to define and limit you. Or, *you* can define the narrative by choosing how to respond to obstacles and challenges. So where does your mind go when challenges come up? How can you become mindful to see the gift of growth and self-discovery that each obstacle brings with it?

As you step into your role as the main character, daring to show up fully, you will experience some pushback! Maybe it's hateful comments, or people not believing in your vision, or family not taking you seriously. If you can mentally prepare yourself for this resistance, being aware that challenges *are* going to come, you can prepare yourself to not feel defeated by them. When you catch yourself wanting to let these obstacles try to take the pen and write your story, keep it firmly in your own hand by responding with gratitude and faith in your vision.

Exercise:

Observe major life events that have defined who you are today. Revisit these key memories. How have your challenges helped you? How might your challenges help others?

Because I experienced
_____ ,
now I can
_____ .

Because I experienced
_____ ,
now I can
_____ .

Because I experienced
_____ ,
now I can
_____ .

QUEST 1 REVIEW

How can your superpowers combine together to serve as a specific career path or lifestyle?

_____

_____

What do you enjoy doing that you wish you could do more of?

_____

_____

What do you hope to create more of in the world?

_____

_____

When you think about the people who inspire you, what does their life teach you?

_____

_____

Summarize in a few sentences how your life experiences can help you and help others.

What would you create with your life story if you knew everyone was rooting for you and your vision?

PART TWO

A Quest to Discover Who I Want to Be

In the first quest, you took the time to observe yourself. You dared to look at yourself in the mirror from new angles, trying on a lens of compassion, finding new purpose in less-than-ideal life experiences. This was all worth your time and thoughtful intention because it laid the foundation for where your story is going to lead next.

In this coming quest, you will use your greatest superpower, your imagination, to define the path you want to pave with your life. You will begin to imagine the kind of main character you want to be. But why exactly is your imagination your greatest tool? Because it allows you to visualize with limitless possibility what you could write in your story. As you paint the picture in your mind, you begin to create expectation and belief in your desired outcomes. By creating this belief in your abilities, so much of the work is already done! For this quest allow yourself to give attention to the dreamer hiding underneath limiting beliefs.

CHAPTER 7

How Can I Dream Up a New Story?

It's time to dream a new story, but first you need to create a foundation for it! When you are intentional about what is influencing the way you think, you can avoid being passively sucked up into the algorithm of what everyone else is telling you to think and become.

Along this quest to become the main character, you're gaining a heightened sense of awareness. You're discovering your power over your reality and your life. In navigating the first quest, you identified how your environment has shaped you up until now. Now you can start to pinpoint areas of your life where you feel pulled in different directions or confused by different voices around you telling you what to be and what to do: Social media, family, friends, community, work, school, etc., are all playing into the way you think. When you take time to separate your own thoughts from the thoughts of these other sources, you can begin to hear yourself a little more clearly and tune in to your true desires. It's time to clear the stage to set up for the next act.

IDENTIFYING DIGITAL HABITS:
WHAT HAPPENS WHEN I UNPLUG?

Technology is an incredible gift full of possibilities. It opens countless doors to connect people and spread ideas in an instant. But could technology be hurting you just as much as (maybe even more than) it's helping? Technology is a newer kind of diet. It will program you to depend on it if you let it, giving you a dopamine hit with each ping of a new message or like, and slowly taking away your ability to focus! How can you be intentional with your technology use, so that it only serves you and the person you want to become? In what ways can you take a step back and create boundaries with your technology? What would you discover about yourself? Would your self-love go up a few notches?

Consider if you mindlessly check your phone all day: You go to bed with it on your nightstand, wake up to it first thing, have it in arm's reach at every moment with the notifications turned on. You're setting yourself up for constant distraction from being present in what you're actually doing, and also distraction from your greater dreams and aspirations through social media comparison and FOMO.

Exercise:

It's up to you what boundary you need to create right now. Plan an afternoon to go through your devices. Turn off notifications that are unessential. Turn off social media notifications altogether. Delete your social media app for a week, or maybe a month—whatever feels like it would be helpful. Unsubscribe to anything unessential. Mute or unfollow accounts that don't make you feel inspired. Practice self-love by creating an environment that will help you be the main character of your life, focused on your unique dreams and goals.

DEFINING PLAY:
IT'S NOT JUST FOR LITTLE KIDS!

"There's no time for play!" says the ego. "Silly ego," says the higher self, "you think your desires come from working harder, but play helps you work smarter!" Most of us don't prioritize play as we get older, because we don't understand how much play actually benefits everything else that we do. Play brings pleasure, sparks creativity, and builds relationships (as it is often something you do with others). Play will help you tap in to your imagination as you begin to dream what you want to create in the story of your life.

Play is also subjective. While traveling and watching sports may be one person's play, another person may love long walks and jamming out on musical instruments with their friends. What play looks like for you could be the most nonsensical thing to someone else. It doesn't need to match anyone else's idea of play. Remember what you learned earlier about romanticizing your life? It means getting lost in the moments of joy and curiosity through play!

Exercise:

Define your play. Think about the activities that make you feel energized, let you lose track of time, and allow you to tap in to curiosity and joy. (Revisit the Identifying Where You Spend Your Time: I Lose Track of Time When I... exercise in Chapter 2.) Where can you fit play into your schedule?

DISCOVERING THE ART OF DOING NOTHING:
THE POWER OF BOREDOM

If play is stimulating and exciting, let's explore the other side of time spent without purpose: boredom. It often feels like we do everything to avoid being bored—to always be entertained. And because most of us have a mini computer in our pocket (a.k.a. a smartphone), it's so easy to scratch the itch to be occupied whenever we feel the slightest sense of boredom. But mindlessly reaching for the entertainment can be a sign that there is something deeper you may be trying to avoid or suppress.

Practices like meditation can help. How? When you designate time to sit and focus on your breath, not only do you benefit from the practice of being present and still with yourself; you also begin to observe the anxieties and troubles that sometimes interrupt your focus. This is how you can identify your most intrusive thoughts and worries. Through practice, you can begin to observe these feelings more comfortably and not tie who you are to them. To be the creator of your future, you must first be the master of your mind!

Exercise:

Try this ten-minute meditation. Sit or lie down in a comfortable spot with your palms out, facing upward. Close your eyes. Spend ten minutes focusing on your breath. Observe the thoughts that occasionally interrupt your focus as you slowly breathe in and out. Become mindful of them, observing that they are only thoughts, then bring your focus back to your breath.

EVALUATING YOUR CURIOSITIES:
WHERE DO MY THOUGHTS LEAD?

What happens if you open your eyes and mind to what is right here—right where you are, right now? What new things might you discover? You can find out by creating a little extra room in your day to practice mindfulness. What is mindfulness exactly? Simply put, it's making yourself very aware of the moment you're in. It's kind of like snapping a mental picture of the present. Mindfulness matters, as the material for creating your dreams is not somewhere out there in the past or future, it's right *here* in this very moment. Are you fully aware in this moment to see the possibilities right in front of you? Or does your mind frequently turn to the past or future?

Whether it's taking a walk and "stopping to smell the roses"; sitting in a favorite spot and tuning in to the smells, sounds, and sights around you; putting your phone away at a meal to really taste your food; or slowing down to journal about what you're feeling, there are so many easy ways to practice mindfulness. When you are present, you notice details, and your curiosity in the here and now allows you to discover new things.

Exercise:

Create moments today to engage your five senses. Observe your surroundings. Inhale deeply and take in smells. Listen to the sounds of the world around you. Taste the flavors of your food. Reach out and touch whatever you can. Feel the feelings that come up. Then give thanks that you can experience all these things with your human body and mind.

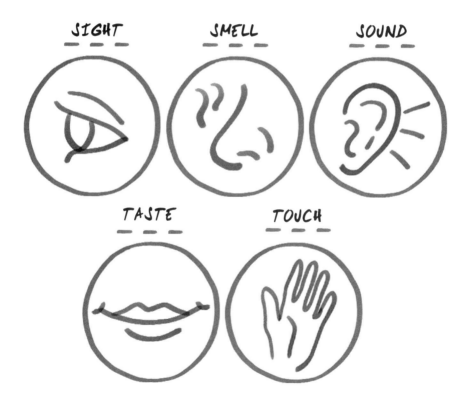

SIGHT   SMELL   SOUND

TASTE   TOUCH

CHAPTER 8

Who Do I Want to Become?

Do you ever visualize yourself doing something before you are about to do it? Maybe before having a difficult conversation you imagine what you will say and how you will respond. Or you imagine yourself eating your favorite take-out food for dinner and then your mouth begins salivating as you recall how delicious it tastes. Or maybe you imagine yourself winning a competition, and find yourself full of adrenaline and confidence as you get ready for it. We use our imagination all the time to create things that aren't tangible yet. Imagination creates a reality inside of us before we ever see it in the physical world. It creates belief and expectation that a certain thing will happen. If we use our imagination with hope, it can bring growth and abundance, helping us rise to the occasion. If we use it with fear, it can cause us to shrink and hold back, anticipating the worst. The belief you create in your imagination affects how you show up to your dreams.

So imagine amazing things! Use your imagination to clarify what it looks like for you to be your best self, walking boldly and purposefully as the main character of your life. It's time to use visualization to help make sure that you show up to your big scenes *ready*.

IDENTIFYING YOUR IDEAL SELF:
MY BEST SELF LOOKS LIKE...

Who is your ideal self—the person you want to become? Take a moment to imagine this person. Flip back to the exercise on defining "main character energy" in the Put Your Rose-Colored Glasses On section and the Identifying What You Want to See More Of exercise in Chapter 3. Reflect on the qualities you value most. How does the "ideal you" carry yourself? What kind of habits do you have? How do you show up to your life day-to-day? To evolve into the main character you want to be, you first need to *imagine* yourself playing your big role. How does this person navigate life...not only the grand moments, but behind the scenes, in the little moments that no one else sees?

Mastering yourself also comes with mastering your emotional world. Consider what percentage of your life is filled with decisions made based on how you feel in the moment. When discouraging thoughts pop into your head—"I'm not motivated!" "I'm too tired," "I'm afraid," or "I don't know how to do it"—how you choose to respond in these moments is what will define your ability to grow. For example, if someone disappointed you, maybe your best self would consider the silver lining to this change of plans and create an open, empathetic conversation to understand the other person's point of view. As you learn to step up when it would definitely be easier to step back, you are beginning to pull back the curtain to discover your best self.

Exercise:

Use your imagination and intuition to finish the following statements. Explain how your best self would respond to these situations.

If someone disappoints me, my best self will:

If I read a hurtful comment, my best self will:

When I am on a walk or car ride by myself, my best self is thinking about:

If something I've worked hard on doesn't pan out, my best self will:

If I don't feel like working on my project, my best self will:

If I feel really stressed and overwhelmed, my best self will:

If someone asks me to do something that I'm not okay with, my best self will:

VISUALIZING YOUR PURPOSE:
HOW DO I SHOW UP FULL OF PURPOSE?

Having a strong sense of purpose makes it a lot easier to take action even when you don't feel like it. Your sense of purpose is the fire under your feet. In the first quest, you began to define your unique purpose by exploring what comes naturally for you and what motivates you. Now you will use your imagination to visualize how your purpose helps define you. How do you see yourself operating out of your purpose? What does it feel like? How does your intention to stay focused on your purpose help you show up every day?

Imagine: You're standing in your future. You're on a stage. It is your moment to shine! There is an audience. Pause for a moment: What are you there to tell them? How will they walk away different because of what you're about to say?

It doesn't matter whether you ever *actually* stand in front of an audience. But whatever you decide to create with your life *is* conveying a message to those around you. Your intention—your "why" that you defined in the previous quest—is your message. So what is it? Maybe you have a vision for how to create change in the educational system. Or how to create better awareness of social injustices. Your own perspective and experiences are what give you a unique voice and story to tell.

Exercise:

Find a comfortable spot where there won't be any disruptions, sit or lie down, and close your eyes. Now start to imagine: What do you want to say with your life? If you don't know what your own "stage" is yet, picture yourself on an actual stage. What would your unique talk be about based on what you know already from your life experiences? And what would you title that talk?

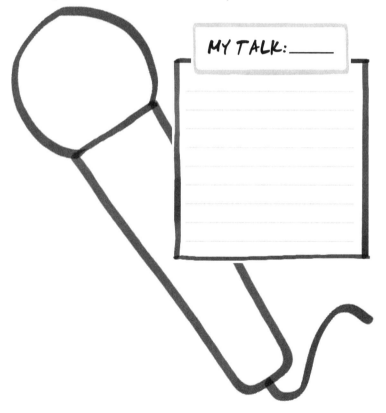

MY TALK: _____

DISCOVERING YOUR CONFIDENCE:
MY BOLD SELF

Being the main character means that you have a strong sense of your worth and your vision. As you journeyed through the first quest in this book, clarity about who you are and what you value was made more tangible. In the past you may have found yourself mindlessly people-pleasing, but now—with a better understanding of what is important to you—you are more mindful to catch yourself in these moments. Standing up for yourself and daring to stand alone call for a real sense of belonging to yourself. Let's practice!

Imagine this: Someone asks you to do something that you are not so comfortable with. It doesn't align with your values in one way or another. You're tempted to go with the flow to avoid an argument or disappointing them...buuut, something deep inside of you feels like you are violating your authentic self if you agree. Consider how you will feel toward yourself later if you do what's easy. Likely, not very good. When you sacrifice integrity toward yourself to avoid a moment of confrontation, you have to live with the results of that choice much longer than that moment itself.

Exercise:

Use your imagination to visualize yourself responding in this kind of situation before it happens. Find a comfortable, quiet spot, sit or lie down, close your eyes, and begin to imagine. You can draw from a past experience or create a new one in your mind. Allow yourself to feel the pressure of this moment. Then take a moment to catch yourself and reflect on the value you have. Consider how staying true to yourself will ultimately benefit you. Then confront the moment. Focus on feeling proud of yourself regardless of how the other person responds.

PRACTICING YOUR CONFIDENCE:
PRACTICE MAKES PERFECT

If your imagination is so powerful that you can begin to believe in the reality you paint in your mind, then you don't actually need the stage, the audience, the instrument, the chessboard, the playing field to practice your craft. By intentionally using your imagination, you can prepare yourself. You can imagine how your fingers will move across the piano, that shot going in on the basketball court, or the steps you need to take to perform a seamless surgery. The *key* here is vividly painting the event in your mind. The more details you imagine, the more real it will feel and the more likely you will be to create an emotional response to the experience. And your emotional world is powerful: It will help you believe this imagined moment is truly happening. So focus on mastering the event. Breathe deeply through your nerves and concentrate on the task. By the time you experience the event in your physical reality, you'll feel like you've done it before. You'll be confident that you can do it again. You'll know you are capable!

Exercise:

Choose the craft you'd like to get better at. Do you want to get better at approaching people? Better at handling the stress of public speaking or performing? Do you want to get better at playing an instrument or game? Once you have your craft, find a comfortable, quiet spot. Sit or lie down, close your eyes, and begin to imagine yourself doing this craft. Be as specific and vivid as possible. Imagine the pressure and feel the adrenaline. Breathe. Coach yourself through the nerves you feel, and practice being completely present, focused, and mastering the experience!

CHAPTER 9

What Do I Want to Create?

Being the main character means taking the risk to show up for yourself, even when it may feel uncomfortable! This is how you will grow and step into the story you desire to write for your life. As you visualized your best self's reaction to different experiences in previous exercises, you began preparing yourself for the important moments that will help propel you toward your dreams. You also began to believe that you are capable and worthy of stepping into these moments. Will feeling able and deserving of the things you want draw them your way? Absolutely! You will begin to make choices that open doors in your desired direction. You will be more confident in your abilities. Now that you've focused on *who* you are going to be, let's focus on *what* you will create with your best life.

By visualizing all the amazing things you will create in your ideal reality, you can make these desires tangible. You will be setting them up in your mind like a memory of the future, rather than an abstract dream. No room for negativity, fear, and disbelief here! Use this intentional, meditative practice of visualization to reach for the moon! Anything is possible in the space of imagination.

VISUALIZING YOUR DREAM LIFE:
MY DREAM LIFE LOOKS LIKE...

The first step to creating the lifestyle you desire is knowing *what* you want. Maybe you have a general idea of your dream home, dream career, or dream relationship. Maybe you haven't wanted to be too specific or set the bar too high *just in case* life doesn't pan out that way. I mean, who wants to be disappointed? The problem is, when you decide to *not* be specific about what you want because you fear that you might get your hopes up, you're not giving yourself a fair shot. In a way, you're neglecting the desires deep down inside of you. By visualizing the best possible outcome in real detail, you give yourself the best chance of achieving your dream.

Imagine you're walking through your home in your ideal future. What do you see? What do you smell? Who greets you? You look out the window; what is outside? You head out to go to do what you love, which is your job. What are you doing? Notice the details you observe. Be as specific as possible. As you engage all your senses and engage positive emotion in this imagined reality, you begin to believe it's possible. You begin to draw it into your physical reality.

Exercise:

Create a detailed memory in the future through visualizing it. Start by finding a comfortable spot where you won't be distracted. Sit or lie down and close your eyes. Picture waking up in your life five years from today. What do you see? Walk through a day in your future life. How do you spend the hours of your day? What positive emotions do you feel toward each moment as you experience it?

VISUALIZING YOUR RELATIONSHIPS:
MY DREAM CONNECTIONS

Okay, be honest with yourself: What good is having *stuff* and *things* without sharing them with other people? If you look closely at your desires—behind the money, the house, the career—chances are that the underlying desire is love and connection in your life. Does that sound right? So consider this: Who are the people that matter most? What kinds of relationships do you want to deepen in your life? What kinds of connections do you want to make? Who do you want to work with or collaborate with? For example, maybe you want to find a partner to start your business with. Or you want to find a romantic partner who has the same values as you and challenges you to be your best self. Maybe you want to develop your relationship with your best friends, or make connections with other entrepreneurs so you can help each other. You can go far alone, but with others, the possibilities are truly infinite!

Exercise:

Consider the relationships you desire in your life. Who do you hope to cross paths with? Who do you want to deepen your relationship with? Who do you want to invest in and collaborate with? Pick one scenario for now. Could it be someone reaching out to you on social media? Crossing paths with your dream partner? Or a current relationship flourishing? Once you have your scenario in mind, find a comfortable, quiet spot. Sit or lie down and close your eyes. Imagine a specific moment of connection as clearly as if you were watching a movie. Visualize what it looks like and feels like through the five senses. Engage with the positive emotions that come up in this moment.

VISUALIZING FUTURE FEELINGS:
I GOT EVERYTHING I WANT, SO AM I HAPPY?

What brings you the most joy? What makes you feel energized and full of wonder? In the first quest you acknowledged the feeling you are trying to get from what you are pursuing. As you practice using your imagination to visualize through the exercises in this chapter, you will uncover more and more of what engages your emotional world. What is *actually* meaningful to you? What will fulfill you?

Think about it. Is it seeing the huge balance in your bank account that makes you emotional, or is it seeing the joy in your family's eyes when you can do something special for them with that money? Is it looking at your social media profile and seeing you have a million followers, or is it the moment when you see how you have made an impact on someone because of something you've posted? Is it seeing your name blown up on a billboard, or feeling proud of yourself for your commitment to your dreams on the days when it looked like nothing would ever pan out?

As you consider what engages your emotions—what is truly meaningful to you—you see that what you accomplish doesn't carry the meaning. The meaning is found in who you are becoming and the paths you are crossing on the journey there.

Exercise:

What do you want people to say about you and your life when you are gone? What do you want to be remembered for? Use your answers to write your own eulogy.

CREATING YOUR FUTURE: A GRATITUDE JOURNAL BY FUTURE ME

What better creates belief in a future outcome than saying "thank you" for something before you see evidence that it will definitely happen? Drawing things into your life is dependent on your expectations, so engaging in gratitude for what you anticipate is a very powerful tool! Not only does it help you become clearer on *what* you want, but you start to feel like it's already yours.

Maybe you're grateful that you will finally be living in a big city. And for the friendships you'll develop there. Or you're grateful that you will be able to find the perfect car in your price range. And that your business will really be picking up. You could be grateful that you will be able to completely revamp your living space. Or that your relationship will be thriving.

Exercise:

Journal about what you are grateful to see unfold in your future. Jot your dreams down. Don't be afraid to be ambitious or too specific! Walk into your future life as you desire it to be, look around, and say "thank you" for what you see. Start with the space here, and continue writing, in your phone or a separate journal, as your gratitude flows.

CHAPTER 10

How Can I Open My Mind to New Possibilities?

Even if you don't feel like a particularly creative person, you *are* a creator. You wake up each day with free will to make decisions, look for solutions to problems, and find ways to navigate this world the best you can. You design your life. You design your relationships. You design how you communicate yourself to others. Life itself is a creative process! In order to step away from just *surviving* and into *thriving*, you must take ownership of your creativity, and find ways to claim it in everything you do.

Creativity is a muscle. The more you exercise your problem-solving skills, the more you'll be able to connect the dots between unlikely things, sparking new ideas! It's time to think outside of the box. To discover how your unique skills and traits can work together to create something original. As you open up the doors in your mind and practice stretching your own creative muscle, you will begin to see things in a new light. You will take the lead in crafting the story of *you*, main character.

FINDING INSPIRATION THROUGH COMMUNICATION: WHEN LANGUAGE IS LIMITING

We spend our whole lives trying to communicate ideas, perspectives, and who we are to others. But what are we saying exactly? And what are others actually hearing? When it comes to communication there are three factors: the words being spoken, the tone they're being said in, and the body language used while they're being said. *What* is being said is often less telling than *how* it is being said—by a whole lot, actually! Most communication happens through the *emotion* in the tone of the person's voice and their body language.

When emotion is utilized well, words can almost become irrelevant. Why do you think music is a universally appreciated art? People across the world jam out to lyrics they don't understand all the time, because how they are sung makes them *feel* something. Have you ever bought something advertised simply because of how it was presented? Did you need it? Or were you moved by the emotional story of how this thing could improve your life?

Maybe your passion is the same as a lot of people's passion. Maybe you feel like a dime a dozen. How can the story you're writing stand out? How can you capitalize on your quirks and find a unique approach to communicate something in a *new* and effective way? Let's exercise this muscle through a hands-on activity.

Exercise:

Pull out your favorite pens/pencils. Put on some music, like an instrumental soundtrack or your favorite song. How would this song look if you could see it on paper? Do you see something abstract or specific? What colors do you see? Draw your interpretation here. There's no wrong answer! Reflect on other ways you can use emotion to communicate.

FINDING SOLUTIONS IN UNLIKELY PLACES: CHANGING MY PERSPECTIVE

When you are able to turn something considered trash into a treasure, you've learned what it's like to be resourceful. You are being artistic with what you have. In a world where we are so used to buying, discarding, and buying again, we have a lot of wasted materials! Our trash is taken away by a garbage truck, so that it ends up out of sight and therefore out of mind. Which means that we don't really see the ripple effects that our small habits create in the world. But we *are* creating the world with our choices every day—whatever they may be. So how can you be intentional with your resources?

You can take small steps in your own story to be resourceful, be it by recycling those jars you always throw in the trash or starting a business that uses resourceful practices. What if there are solutions in the very things you discard? What if there is potential hiding in something unexpected...potential you could never see unless you went looking? Do you have an eye open to the hidden solutions? Can you see possibilities in unlikely places? Treasures are often not where you'd expect them to be.

Exercise:

Identify objects that you might normally discard. How could they be given a second life? Perhaps broken pottery could be turned into a mosaic, ribbons from packaging reused to make hair ties, candle jars turned into planters, or coffee grounds used as food for your garden. What can you come up with? Look around you and ask yourself, "Could this be given a second life?" You don't have to start making masterpieces, but identifying the many possibilities that live inside what you already have will help you to begin seeing more possibilities around you.

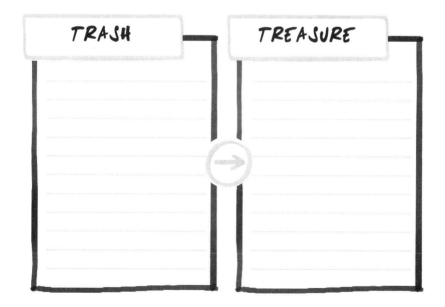

TRASH

TREASURE

DISCOVERING THE POWER
OF INNOVATION:
WORKING WITH LIMITED
RESOURCES

What if the limitation you've felt in your life is actually *to your advantage*? A limit in resources forces you to exercise your creativity and find less-than-obvious ways to use what you already have. Often, it's not until a situation of survival or crisis occurs that we are forced to think outside of the box. But what if your innovative idea is just on the other side of experimenting with your resources now?

Imagine: You have been eyeing a piece of artwork for a long time. But it's so expensive! You decide to make your own version with the things you own. It's a risk, as it might turn out terribly. But you begin experimenting with the materials you already have. You have some paints and papers. Even some random objects and glue. You begin painting, gluing down objects, adding crumpled papers for texture, etc. You create something quirky and original. Now your friends ask you to make them one too. You get more requests. Next thing you know, you've started a business! Working with what you had on hand opened you to a whole new world. Consider: Could there be more potential in what you already have? Could there be more potential in *you*?

Exercise:

Find three random objects around you (they can be anything: a paperclip, a rubber band, a small rock, etc.). Observe the items and how the materials could work together. What could you create? See how many different ideas you come up with. Write down each invention here. It may feel kind of like child's play, but this practice will help you exercise your ability to discover more creative solutions in working with what you have. After all, your imaginative inner child may have something important to teach you!

My Invention

My Invention

My Invention

My Invention

CHAPTER 11

How Can I Motivate Myself to Take Action?

In getting ready to take action as the main character of your life, you have to set the stage of your environment so that it suggests the story you want to tell. The way you keep your home, what you surround yourself with, what music is playing in the background, and what you look at and visually absorb regularly all influence your subconscious mind. They influence your choices and habits. They affect the way you *feel* every day. So it's important to create a sanctuary that inspires you in the direction of your dreams.

Consider that the room or home you live in is an external representation of your internal world. You tell the story of who you are through your knickknacks, your cleanliness (or lack thereof), and the colors and patterns you choose. So if it is a reflection of who you are, that means you can also utilize your environment to help you become who you want to be. What do you observe in the environment you've created? Is there neglect anywhere? Is there a lack of intention? Are there temptations or distractions lingering in plain sight? Creating intention in this external space is an easy place to start creating more intention in your life as a whole.

CREATING YOUR VISION BOARD:
LOOKING AT MY "WHY"

If you only take the time to do one crafty or artsy thing in your life, let it be creating a vision board for yourself. (Why was this not a requirement in school?!) What is a vision board? It's a collection of images and words you put together into a collage of what you want. A vision board can be for anything from a dream career or huge party you are planning, to a vision for who you want to become and what you want to achieve in your life. In order for it to work, it needs to be placed somewhere you will see it on a regular basis. Your vision board works by not only reminding you of *what* to focus on, but also by suggesting to your subconscious mind that what you see on the board is your reality (just not yet in physical form!). Your desires become more than a hopeful idea; you begin to really believe that they will come to pass. And belief is a powerful substance that compels you to take action.

So what should be the focus of your vision board? It can be anything that you hope for: your dream home, the family you want to have, that podcast you want to start, yourself on that stage, your business booming. Get as specific as you can and, by all means, reach for the stars.

Exercise:

Pull images and words from magazines, Google, and/or Pinterest. Put them together in a collage on a poster board, inside a large frame or lookbook, or stitched together as the wallpaper on your phone or laptop. Put time and thought into this. Enjoy the process of curating it—this is exciting stuff!

CREATING AN INSPIRING SPACE: A SUGGESTIVE AMBIENCE

In the same way that a vision board can suggest your desired future and help you begin the process of manifesting your dreams, so can everything else you use to decorate your space. The art on your walls, the books on display, the colors you use and how those colors make you feel—all of these visual elements tell the story of *you*, and continually reinforce to your subconscious mind who you are. So are you suggesting the story of who you *want* to be?

If you want to live somewhere specific, hang a poster or large photograph or painting of that place. If you want to read more regularly, display books where you will see them and be inspired to read. If you want to make healthy meals, curate a menu to put on the fridge or make a recipe book of your favorite meals and keep it in the kitchen. Google *color psychology*. If you want to feel warmth and optimism, bring in gold or yellow. If you want to feel clean, utilize the simplicity of white. Do you want to feel grounded? Add greens to your home—plants are an obvious choice. What do you want more of in your life? Suggest it through the details and ambience of your space.

Exercise:

Identify what you will put more intention behind in curating your environment to create an ambience that suggests the way you want to feel and the life you want to create. Be practical! You don't need to break the bank. Use your creativity like you practiced in the previous chapter. Make the changes doable for you.

FORGING VISUAL FOCUS:
TIDYING MY SPACE AND MIND

In with the new means out with the old! You identified where you want to be intentional in the ambience of your space to suggest the life you desire. Now, in order to really focus on what you want to create and take action on it, you need to *clear out the clutter*. Let's start with the clutter in your environment.

What could be holding you back in your surroundings? Are certain mementos holding you in the past and keeping you from moving on to the you that you want to become? Are there clothes in your closet that are more in your way than they are sources of pleasure and confidence? Are you holding on to something because it cost you a lot, but it doesn't fit with your life anymore? Are there songs on your playlist that take you to past memories you need to move on from? (Scents can have the same effect.) If something in your environment doesn't suggest the person you want to become, it's going to distract you from making progress to become that person. Create clarity of mind by giving yourself some blank space, *a clean slate*. Creating intention in every area of your life is a true practice of self-love.

Exercise:

Take a look around your space. Make a pile of anything that is not a favorite thing. Now get rid of the things you have any lukewarm feelings about and don't need. Clear out the passive areas of your life so you have room for your 100 percent intention.

QUEST 2 REVIEW

Where am I creating room in my life to daydream and play?

_____

_____

I would describe my best, ideal self as:

_____

_____

What I want to create with my life includes (this is what goes on your vision board!):

_____

_____

I want to be remembered for being:

_____

_____

_____

My "limitations" serve me by helping me to come up with unique and innovative ways to get where I want to go. For example:

How am I curating my environment to support who I want to become?

PART THREE

A Quest to Become That Person

You have gone through two quests of self-discovery: first, creating awareness of who you are and what you value. Next, creating awareness of who you want to become and what you want to create with your life. Or, rather, who you *will* become and what you *will* create (remember: the words you use are important!). Now it's time to become that person and create those things by building healthy habits, boundaries, and internal rewards into your lifestyle. The main character is intentional with their time, energy, and resources so that they can achieve what they have set their mind to.

The path to your best life is laid on a foundation of practicing mindfulness and gratitude every step of the way, taking ownership of what you can control, and letting go of what you can't. It is a path of inner freedom, finding the courage to be true to who you are, and going on a new and exciting adventure. (And the main character is always up for adventure!)

CHAPTER 12

What Attitude Will Help Me Thrive?

Why is your attitude such an important element to your success on this journey? Consider what makes for a "bad attitude": ungratefulness, entitlement, and negativity. How do you feel being around other people who have those attitudes? What about people who are grateful, positive, and make *you* feel important? Don't you want to see people with those attitudes become leaders and influencers? Don't you want to be around those kinds of people? Truly, a good attitude can open doors that talent and work ethic alone never could.

Not only does a good attitude give you leverage with others, but, most importantly, it benefits the way *you* experience life. It is the lens through which you process events as they happen. A good lens means a good life! Recall what it means to "romanticize" your life. Remember: A positive attitude is born in *mindfulness*. When you look through a lens of gratitude, you become aware that each step of your journey is there to teach you something valuable, preparing you for the steps ahead. Gratitude will help you stay out of the comparison game and give you the grit you need for your journey.

CREATING A THANKFUL ATTITUDE:
TODAY IS A GOOD DAY

Practicing gratitude is like opening your arms to say "thank you!" and life responding by throwing back even more to be thankful for. Whatever circumstances you find yourself in, look for what the situation has to offer you. On the good days *and* on the hard days, look for what you can gain from every single experience. As you begin to make "thank you" a habitual utterance, you'll start to notice the positives before the negatives. You'll start to feel abundant. And that will create even more abundance in your life. Gratitude is the gift that keeps on giving. It transforms your mental health, inherently transforming your physical health, and ultimately transforming your life. Seriously, if you want to improve your health in any regard, start with gratitude.

Consider this: According to research, the chance of you existing at all is one in four hundred *quadrillion*. (Maybe take a minute just to let that one sink in!) When you look at your life with that in mind, any petty detail about the way you look or your personality becomes almost irrelevant; the import-ant thing is that you *exist!* You have already been chosen. You have beaten so many odds. And here you are in *this* moment in time—with breath in your lungs, ready to experience life. You have the creativity inside of you to make something with today.

Exercise:

Take a deep breath in; feel your lungs fill with air, and observe your surroundings. Point out what you are grateful for. Think about the people in your life who have helped you get where you are today. What have they made possible for you? Consider the challenges you are currently facing. How are they teaching you invaluable lessons? In this present moment, what do you get to enjoy through your senses?

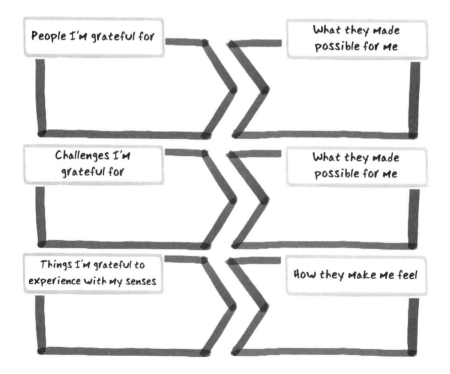

People I'm grateful for

What they made possible for me

Challenges I'm grateful for

What they made possible for me

Things I'm grateful to experience with my senses

How they make me feel

LEARNING TO ACT THROUGH A LENS OF SERVICE:
GENEROSITY

In the previous exercise, who were the people who came to your mind that helped you get to where you are today? What did they give you that absolutely *melts* you with gratitude? How did they invest in who you have become? Their life lives beyond them, *inside of you* and in the story you will write. In the same way, your life can go beyond you, in the way that *you* invest in others.

Test this theory. Ask someone who has lived a long life and chased many things what was most fulfilling for them. Is it what they did for someone else? Are the people in their life what made it rich and meaningful rather than the prestige or the glamour? This is a common question and one worth learning from. How can you invest in others in the same way that others have invested in you? How can you leave a legacy behind with the story you are writing?

Exercise:

Consider how you can make generosity a habit in your life. Could you be more thoughtful in your approach toward your work or school? Could you set alerts on your phone to reach out to your friends, or surprise someone with a thoughtful gift? Do you have an outlet to offer your skills through volunteering or doing favors? Reflect on what you have to give: time, resources, skills, a listening ear. Write your intentions here. In what ways can you be a supporting character in others' lives?

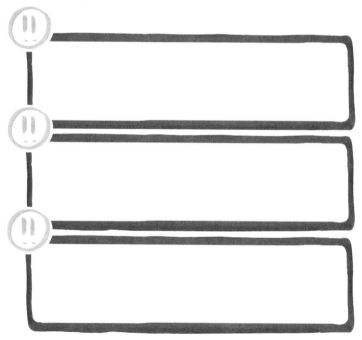

BUILDING A SUPPORT SYSTEM:
HELPING OTHERS AND BEING HELPED

Generosity toward others will build relationships in your life. It's a good thing too: You weren't designed to travel this life journey alone. A great main character always has a team of supporting characters. Taking the journey—writing the story—*together* is what makes it rich. How? Other people have resources, skills, and perspectives you don't have. And you have things they don't have! There is so much to learn from others, and they have so much to learn from you.

Let's be real. What is the most challenging thing in life? *Relationships*. What is the most fulfilling thing in life? *Relationships*. They are challenging because they are designed to make us better—more self-aware, thoughtful, and resilient. They are fulfilling because all of us are limited on our own. Look around you. Everything in the world shares a relationship to everything else. Everything depends on something else to exist, serve its purpose, and keep the balance. We are designed to support one another!

Exercise:

Identify who you are supporting. How can you promote and uplift them and the story they are writing? For example, maybe a friend is starting a new business. Could you give them a shout-out on social media? Or offer your time and abilities to help them? Maybe they are interested in making more connections. Why not introduce them to some of your other friends? Jot down what makes your friend unique and valuable as if you were putting an ad out for them. This will help you think about how you can encourage them and who you can connect them with to help them reach their dreams and write their story. It's so much more fun doing life together.

MY FRIEND IS AMAZING!

VALUING COMMUNITY OVER COMPETITION: CELEBRATING EVERYONE'S SUCCESS

As you discover your unique purpose, and realize that no one else can be you, as you see the value in each step of your own journey, and trust the timing of how your story will unfold, as you trust that the things you desire you truly are capable of having—this is when you can find yourself less threatened by the success of others and more *inspired* by it. After all, if they can do it, *perhaps you can too!*

If someone else's success threatens your own access to success, you are believing that there is a limited amount of success, resources, ideas—you name it—in the world. This belief will cause you to think and act out of stinginess and… well, life will be stingy back. It's essentially feeling like someone else stole your story, and now you can't write your own. Which is not true, because no one is you! And you have something important to say in only the way that *you* can. What if you could even see someone else's success as your own? What if the story wasn't you *against* them, but you *with* them? How different would you feel about your life? What would come from that? Abundance attracts abundance! Really, the only thing you need to compete with is the stinginess that wants to keep you small.

Exercise:

Think of someone you know who you might be jealous of and/or find threatening. Rather than following your first instinct to be stingy toward them, what if you did the opposite and showed generosity? Send them a message to let them know how they inspire you. Promote them on social media. Even if generosity is not your first instinct, let your action precede your feelings and watch it begin to shift your own story!

Initial Feelings   Action

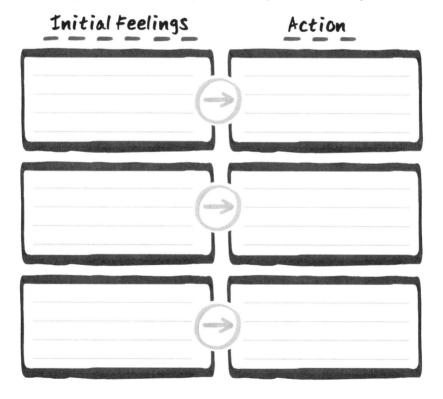

CHAPTER 13

What Boundaries Will Get Me Where I Need to Go?

Investing in relationships is an invaluable part of your journey. But where do you draw the line between being there for others and straight-up people-pleasing? It takes honest self-awareness and self-love to confidently create boundaries in your life. You have to know what you want and what you *don't* want, and then have the courage to follow through on those boundaries, even if they irritate someone else every now and again. Boundaries reflect your ability to see your own worth and respect it.

Creating boundaries will help keep you on track in the direction toward the life you want to live. True, boundaries can feel uncomfy and confrontational at first, but the long-term result is an intentional life that you're proud of and can enjoy. *Not* creating boundaries is leaving a door wide open for resentment to enter in. For everything you say yes to, you are saying no to other things. Are you saying no to your own inner peace? Let's find out.

ESTABLISHING YOUR BOUNDARIES:
I CAN'T DO IT ALL

You may want to be everything to everyone. It's tempting, that's true. After all, it's easy to associate making others happy with being a good person. But could you be spreading yourself too thin, making it hard to have enough of yourself to give in order to make actual progress where it counts?

Consider that (a) you have a finite amount of energy, focus, and time that you are responsible for managing, and (b) no one else can see the vision you have for your life like you can. When you are intentional with what you devote your energy to, you protect your vision and mission. You become less prone to overcommitting and finding yourself depleted and resentful toward others for asking so much of you. Look at it this way: When you make your life choices based on how others will think of you versus how *you* will think of you, you are making yourself less respectable (because you're not respecting yourself!), wearing down your own integrity (because you are being inconsistent toward yourself!), and trading in being true to your big dream for small bites of quick external validation (because maybe you don't fully trust that your vision *will actually* pan out!).

Exercise:

Identify the time that you have control over in your life. Consider your purpose, what you value, and what feels like the best use of that time and your energy. List these priorities in the large circle. Determine any unwelcome triggers of guilt, people-pleasing, or passive distractions like scrolling through social media that try to steal your focus away from those important things and affect your inner peace. List these distractions in the smaller circles. Taking time to become aware of these things will help you know when a boundary is needed.

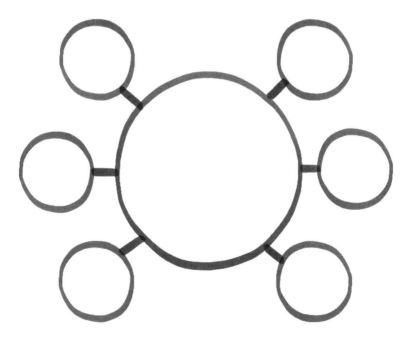

IDENTIFYING DECISION FATIGUE:
SETTING MYSELF FREE WITH LIMITATION

Boundaries act like the road on a map, helping to direct you to the destination you have in mind. When you take the time to define what these boundaries are and commit to them, you protect yourself from "decision fatigue." This kind of fatigue hits you when you are making so many decisions that you start to lose the energy and focus necessary to make beneficial decisions. Instead, you're likely to make decisions that aren't super thought-out—or avoid decisions altogether! While the idea of intentionally creating limitations for yourself may sound restrictive, the fact is that endless possibility and freedom can be straight-up overwhelming and leave you feeling paralyzed. When you create structure so that you can be consistent, you can gain more momentum toward where you want to go!

Let's say you want to be healthy. It's one thing to aim toward an indefinite goal of "trying to make healthy decisions"; it's another thing to intentionally decide that you will say no to desserts or processed snacks. It's one thing to say, "I want an enjoyable morning routine"; it's another thing to enforce a specific bedtime. One is vague and doesn't offer a clear place to start; the other gives the details for exactly how you will meet your goal. Where do *you* need to define limitations so you can focus on creating and becoming who you want to be?

What specific limitations will you create for yourself to prevent decision fatigue and getting stuck along the way to your goals? In the space provided along the map, list ways you can set limits that will help you stay on course.

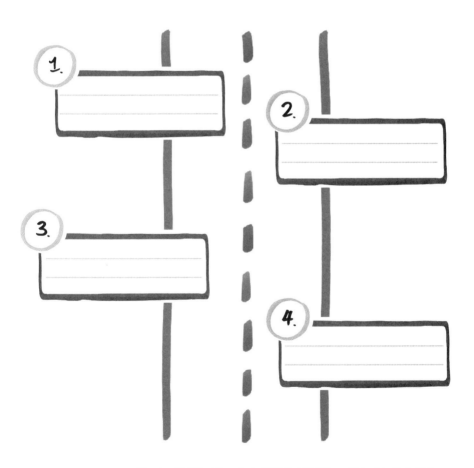

PRACTICING SELF-RESPECT:
I AM FREE TO DISAPPOINT

What is the consequence of having boundaries? You may not be as "nice" as others thought you were (a.k.a. an "exhausted people-pleaser"), but you will discover a greater capacity for love in your life. Why? When you love yourself enough to respect yourself through upholding boundaries, you will treat others with that same respect. And they will respect you for respecting yourself. Though you may not appear as nice to some, you will actually *be* a better person—more trustworthy and on a sustainable path toward reaching your dreams.

Anticipate it. Living with intention means that you *will* disappoint people. You will ruffle some feathers. Instead of seeing that confrontational moment as a loss, see it as a win. You stood up for yourself! You grew a little taller. You endured a little discomfort, and now you can experience the long-term bliss of doing what is best for you and healthiest for your relationships.

Exercise:

Create a system of accountability when responding to a request. Ask yourself: "If I say yes, am I saying it out of fear? Or am I saying it out of love?" Likewise, "If I say no, am I saying it out of fear? Or am I saying it out of love?" Be honest about the intention that surfaces. For example, maybe someone asks you to watch their pet. Are you wanting to say yes because you want them to think you are helpful, even though you are already busy with other responsibilities? If you are operating from fear of upsetting or disappointing someone, you are setting yourself up for resentment. Ask this question to create boundaries that will help you love yourself and others well.

Fear (or) Love?

I'm acting passive; playing a small role.

I'm acting intentional; stepping up to the main character role.

CHAPTER 14

What Habits Will Get Me Where I Need to Go?

Defining your boundaries has been a starting point for creating intention. Your boundaries protect the time and energy that you need to create your dreams. Now, how will you manage that time and energy?

In the last quest, you imagined yourself living the life of your dreams, being the best version of you. You can see in your mind the person you want to become! Now it's time to identify what actions you must take. In order to become that person, you must begin to *act* like that person. What kinds of habits does this person have? How do they spend their free time? What do they eat? Who do they hang out with? What do they think about? You can't change your entire life overnight, but you can start to make micro changes in your behavior that will build up into bigger changes over time. All big things start small. The most successful person you can think of was once a beginner in their field. Trust the power of small beginnings and small choices!

IDENTIFYING ACTION STEPS:
SLOW GROWTH IS SUSTAINABLE GROWTH

From the outside looking in, it can seem like some people become a success overnight. One day they're a normal person, the next, a superstar! Most of the time it doesn't actually happen that fast; it just looks that way. While you may see a person with fame and fortune, what you didn't see were the years during which they refined their skills and got clear on their vision through practice and mistakes.

When you look at your own desires, you might feel overwhelmed thinking about the space between what your life looks like right now and what you want it to look like. So rather than focusing on the outcome of what you want to achieve, focus on behaving like the kind of person who would get there. What kind of habits does this person have? For example, consider the journey of an icon like Walt Disney. As a teenager, he had a dream to be a newspaper cartoonist when he grew up. In order to work toward that goal, he started taking art classes and pursuing opportunities such as drawing for his high school newspaper. He would later discover animation, be inspired by a mouse, and imagine something that had never been done before. As he focused on taking action in the best way he knew how, doors opened, more ideas came, and confidence in his abilities grew. What are some habits *you* could begin implementing to take action?

Exercise:

Identify three of your goals/desires, then name a small action step you can begin taking today that will help bring each desire to life. Finally, determine the time and place that you will show up to begin practicing each of these habits. Be realistic and specific, so that you can add this action into your schedule and follow through.

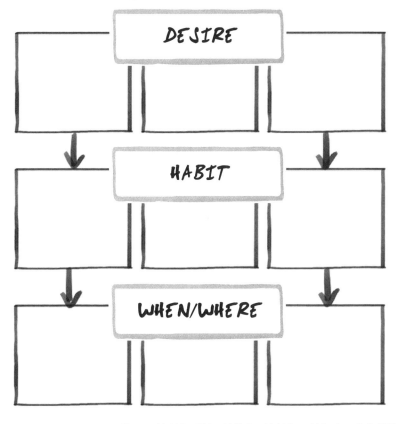

FOCUSING ON DIRECTION VERSUS GOALS:
STAY FLEXIBLE AND ADAPTABLE

Knowing what your goals are allows you to figure out what steps you need to take and what habits to implement to get you moving in the right direction. And in your day-to-day thinking, that's all you really need to focus on: *moving in the right direction.* Getting too fixated on a specific goal can lead you to focus on external results that you ultimately can't control. What you *can* control is yourself, and showing up for yourself every day. You won't be able to predict curveballs, new opportunities, or changes. But you can hold on to the clarity of your "why" and take small steps in the direction of this passion.

Think about goals you've set in your past. Did you expect that you would *finally* be happy when you achieved them? But by the time you actually reached that goal, you were probably thinking about the next goal, right? Goals can make us future-focused, and cause us to lose mindfulness and gratitude in the present moment. So how can you find satisfaction in just moving in the direction of your dreams? For example, say you want to run a marathon so you can feel like you're capable of accomplishing hard things. While training for the marathon, focus on how you are proving that you are already capable of accomplishing hard things, as you show up consistently to go for long runs.

Exercise:

Write down your goals and the desired feeling behind each one. Why do you want it? Consider how you can achieve that desire in the journey and process of working toward your goal.

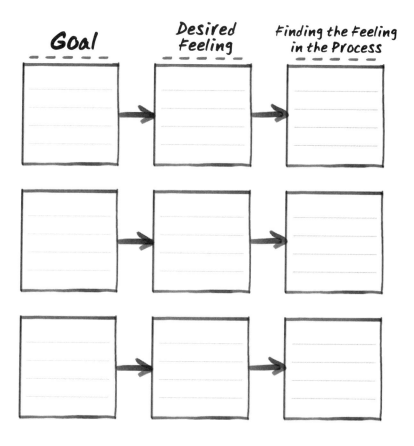

Goal   **Desired Feeling**   **Finding the Feeling in the Process**

MAKING HARD HABITS EASIER:
HABIT STACKING, BUT FUN

What do you think of when you hear the word *habits*? Do you think of your bad habits? Do you think of something that sounds like a good idea, but you can't ever seem to stick to it when you try? In this exercise, you're going to learn how to make the positive but *not so easy* habits easier for you to maintain in your day-to-day.

Let's say you want to be someone who works out five times a week or who regularly practices a certain instrument or who reads a book every month, but it's always a battle to keep at it. You never feel like doing it. Maybe you even feel defeated after the first time trying. In the last quest you focused on creating an environment that supports the behavior you want to have. Now you need to create a reward system to set yourself up for success. Creating a good experience around the act of doing the habit will make it easier to stick to it. If a habit is difficult, associate it with something pleasurable by following it up with a rewarding routine—something that gives you that dopamine hit your body wants. Turn the hard habits into rewarding rituals. For example, at eight a.m. when you run one mile around your neighborhood, put on your favorite playlist that puts you in a good mood for the day. Then when you finish your run, treat yourself by making a tasty smoothie for breakfast.

Exercise:

Identify five hard habits you would like to include in your lifestyle. Then list the pleasurable habits that you can attach as a reward for doing each hard habit.

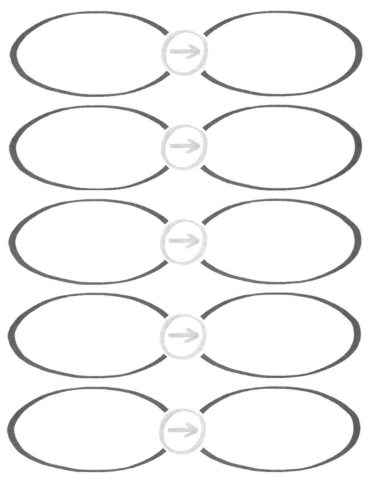

BUILDING CONFIDENCE BY KEEPING PROMISES TO YOURSELF:
I WON'T CANCEL ON MYSELF

Wherever you are on the spectrum of feeling confident, as you start becoming more and more consistent in your desired habits you will find your self-confidence growing. Why? You'll have evidence that you *can* do what you set your mind to! Confidence is born from keeping promises to yourself. Making a list, setting an agenda, creating a visual plan, and going about checking off the items as you complete them is a powerful tool to build your confidence and map out your priorities.

Time is a resource everyone has; creatively managing that time to serve you is *key*. Whether you're a night person or a morning person, introvert or extrovert—consider your own clock and work with it. When do you have the most energy? When are you most creative? When are you better at hands-on tasks? And when are you better at thinking tasks? Organizing your tasks so they match your natural flow of energy will help you be most efficient. Start with tasks that are most time sensitive or that you feel the most resistance toward acting on. If you can get those out of the way, you will feel like you're winning, and you'll find yourself with more capacity and energy to do the less urgent tasks that may excite you more.

Exercise:

On a separate piece of paper, make a list of everything you want to do today or this week. Put a star next to your top three tasks. After the top three tasks, number the other things you'd like to get to-if possible-in order of importance. Then make your agenda. Couple the harder tasks with pleasurable habits (a dance or coffee break, a mindfulness walk, etc.). Use the following example to help you make your agenda.

To Do List:

- - - - - - - - - - - - -

★ **Email boss** then enjoy a coffee.

★ **Create project outline** then take a five-minute dance break.

★ **Edit YouTube video** then walk the dog.

5. **Read a chapter** with favorite hot tea.

4. **Clear out email** then have a yummy dinner.

CHAPTER 15

When Do I Take Control and When Do I Let Go?

You've lived long enough to know that life is unpredictable and full of change. And that's what makes for an exciting story! Your ability to adapt is your ability to be a resilient, show-stopping main character. How do you do that? Learning to dance with your circumstances: taking control of what you can control, letting go of what you can't, and trusting in the bigger picture.

Hiding in your bedroom, expecting the phone to ring with your dream opportunity, is passive and probably won't amount to much. (How can an opportunity come if no one knows you exist?!) Trying to control others, the traffic, whether someone will love you or not, and every single detail of every single moment is pure insanity. These are things outside of your control. But you can always control yourself. You can control your perspective, your attitude, the thoughts you meditate on, whose opinion you value, and your willingness to show up. You can find peace knowing in your heart that you've done your best with what is within your power. Hey, maybe that unexpected curveball is leading you just where you need to go.

IDENTIFYING BELIEFS THAT LEAD TO ACTION:
THE FIRST STEP IS IN MY MIND

It's one thing to discover that the story you've been telling yourself isn't serving who you want to become. It's another thing to actively tell a new story through consistent self-suggestion and positive affirmations. Your behavior will always seek to match your personal sense of identity, so if you believe you're a healthy person, for example, you will likely make healthy choices. And if you believe you're a lazy person, you will likely behave like a lazy person. You will look for what you already believe to be true, and that's what you will find and create more of.

So let's take action on informing the internal narrative that gets you to where you want to be. Flip back through the first and second quests and reflect on your answers for who you want to be before completing this exercise.

Exercise:

Use the following space to write out your own daily affirmation that says who you are (the best version of you). For example: "I love the way I look, I love the way I think, and I appreciate how my uniqueness brings value to my work and relationships. Today I am free to tell the truth. I am free to show up as all of me. I will finish the things I start, even if they are imperfect. Today I will make choices that will serve me well tomorrow." Once you have your affirmation, rewrite it neatly on a separate piece of paper and put it somewhere you look every day. Frame it if you want! Or you can record the affirmation on your phone so you can listen to it whenever you need to-whatever will be most meaningful for you.

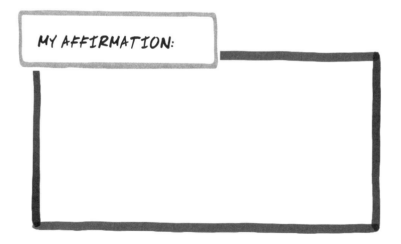

MY AFFIRMATION:

LEARNING TO TAKE INITIATIVE:
GET UP AND GO!

What comes to mind when you think of creating your own opportunity? Sometimes creating your own opportunity is as simple as leaving your house. Or making eye contact with someone and sparking a conversation. You don't know what will come from showing up in the world and being a part of it. But what about when you're not interacting with others? You're at home and you have free time: You could make it some more *Netflix* and chill time *ooor* you could start writing your own movie!

Recall your visualization in the second quest. What did you see yourself doing? And what can you do right now with what you have to take one step in the direction you want to go? Let's say, for instance, you do want to produce movies someday. Where's a place you can start right now to create your own opportunity with what you have? Maybe you have a bedroom for the location, two friends who love to act, a smartphone camera, a mic, a friend who writes, a free weekend to film, and a *YouTube* channel to share your video. That's plenty of resources to start acting on your dream.

Plan what you will create with what you have. Write down what you want to create in the box, then brainstorm the resources you have in the circle. Create more circles around your resource list to plan how you will use those resources.

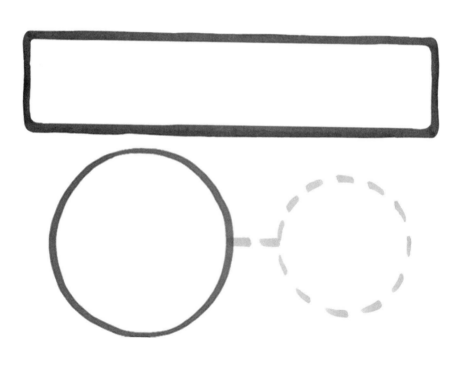

DISCOVERING YOUR OWN PATH:
WORK SMARTER, NOT HARDER

Have you heard of the 80-20 Rule? It's a principle often used in business to explain how just 20 percent of your input leads to 80 percent of your results. In other words, you need to do something a lot before you can see what is actually working for you. We all love quality, buuut it's quantity that *leads* to quality. While 80 percent of your work may feel like it was a waste, because only 20 percent really moved the needle for you, it wasn't a waste! It was essential. You were learning and discovering what your 20 percent is. When you determine your 20 percent (your most useful and efficient efforts), you can start to work smarter, not harder.

Reflect on your life and any areas where you've seen progress. What has been the 20 percent that made a difference? Maybe you've discovered that you do better on school tests when you review your notes for ten minutes every day for a week versus cramming all of your studying into the day before the test. Maybe this same strategy could help you learn a new language. It's less time, and you actually see growth. In what areas have you learned how to work smarter instead of harder, and how can you translate it to your current goals?

Exercise:

In the previous exercise, you brainstormed one thing you could create with your resources. In this exercise, you will consider a variety of things you could create. Think about your variables: What stories do you have to tell? What life experiences do you have? What materials can you work with? Who do you know that can help you? Write down your ideas in the following space. Star or circle your favorite ones (these may be your 20 percent ideas!).

LEARNING TO BE A "GOOD BEGINNER":
IT'S NEVER TOO LATE TO START DOING WHAT I WANT TO DO

Would you do things differently if you could go back in time? If you were younger? Does it feel like it's "too late"? But what if it isn't? What if the opinions or obstacles you're afraid of didn't even exist? What if anything really is possible—regardless of what's "normal" or glorified in society and causes you to think things like "I should be further along by now," "People are not going to take me seriously," or "That would be crazy: I already paid thousands for a degree in something else!" Is there a curiosity inside of you to try something, change something, or start from scratch? It's okay to be a beginner. Even if that means completely changing the plot of the story you thought you were writing. While your change in course may appear like a setback to someone else, it actually puts you light years ahead when you dare to be authentic and honor your deepest desires.

Say you take action on your desire to make a change or start something new: Consider how much progress you could make in five years. Picture your future self looking back five years after choosing to explore the desire, versus looking back after choosing not to. There is no reason to live with the thought "I wish I would have…" for the rest of your life!

Close your eyes and imagine there's no age construct for what you should and shouldn't be doing. You could start acting at forty-five, start a business at sixty, pick up a new instrument in your thirties—how old you are or what your current story is doesn't matter! With that in mind, consider things you would try and things you would change. Write them here. Star the desires that stand out to you the most.

Want to change
- - - - -

Want to try
- - - - -

LOOKING PAST FEAR:
LIVING MY MOST COURAGEOUS LIFE LOOKS LIKE...

Courage means stepping up when you'd really rather step back. The only way to truly grow and create a new story that doesn't look like your past is to do things *differently* than you've done them before. You are going to have to step into the unknown. Not knowing how things will turn out can be a very uncomfortable place to be. But you can definitely know that as soon as you feel the discomfort, if you step into it, you *will* grow. You *will* discover something new.

Choosing courage is feeling your fear, imposter syndrome, nervousness, unworthiness, and everything else that bubbles up, and still *showing up* to the scene to put your best foot forward. What gives you the ability to do this? The painful memory of playing a passive role—of being a background character—weighs heavier than the discomfort of showing up to this vulnerable moment as the main character. Because even if you totally mess up, you will be a different person than you would be if you'd never even tried. Isn't that worth it? Give yourself a shot. Nothing will boost your confidence like facing your fears.

Exercise:

What have you been afraid of and avoiding doing, even though deep down you really want to do it? Confronting a friend about a boundary they crossed? Signing yourself up for a class that will force you to practice public speaking? Reaching out to someone you're interested in? Trying to get a gig to perform your song? Auditioning for that play? Write down the things that scare you, then show them who is boss. Go back to the visualization technique in the second quest of this book and visualize yourself stepping into your fear and mastering it.

Actions That Will Help Me Grow:

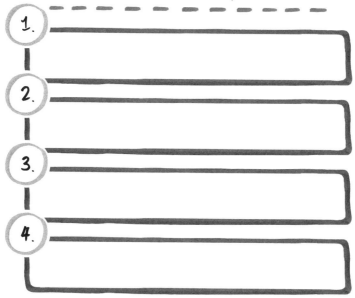

1.

2.

3.

4.

FINDING THE COURAGE
TO BE YOURSELF:
WHEN I AM ~~PERFECT~~ SEEN, I AM LOVABLE

Why do you think you have the fears you named in the previous exercise? What makes some things scary is how vulnerable you feel when you step into something where you can't control the outcome. Maybe it's making another attempt at something that didn't go well in the past. Or maybe it's just something you are uncomfortable with but want to try because you know it could make a big difference. To put yourself "out there," to potentially be seen as less than perfect, or even a miserable failure, feels like a huge risk.

But think about the people you love. Don't you love them for the wholeness of who they are? Don't you love them regardless of what they aren't perfect at? In fact, when they let you see parts of their life that look less than perfect, it actually helps you connect with them more because you can share in your challenges. We love people who we can relate to in our own humanity. We love them despite and often *because* of their imperfections.

So the key is not to be perfect. The key is to own where you're at in your journey. Admit you're nervous. Admit it's your first time. Admit you're struggling. Let the audience empathize with you as you step into uncharted territory. Your courage to own your fear will inspire others.

Exercise:

What are the vulnerable parts of you that you don't want others to see? Write a letter of encouragement to someone else who is experiencing the same fear and shame that have held you back. Let them know how you are working to show up even in your fear, because you know it will lead to an amazing story.

You Aren't Alone and Neither Am I

Sincerely, _____

COMPETING AGAINST YOURSELF:
FOCUSING ON THE BIGGER PICTURE

You can compete against others and always find that they have something you don't, ooor you can focus on what *you* have and compete with your past self in the hopes of being better today than you were yesterday. One competition is going to be a lot more rewarding than the other.

It's much easier to compete against yourself instead of others when you take a bird's-eye view of your life's story. Right now, you may be fully consumed by how life feels and how those around you might perceive the path you're on. But consider this: Someday you are going to be old and gray. Time will have passed; maybe by this time you will have kids or grandkids sitting around you, wanting to hear your story. What *kind* of story do you want to tell them? Definitely not the one where you ended up working a job you hated for forty years just so someone else would think you were successful. Or the one where you spent half of your life comparing yourself to other people, only to feel worse and worse about who you are and what you are doing.

Exercise:

Write a letter from your future self to your past self, thanking you for focusing on your own growth, having patience with yourself, and giving yourself a shot at your dreams. Write about the life that you've been able to live because you chose to believe in yourself even when others weren't supportive of your dream or it seemed like the odds of succeeding were not in your favor.

Dear Past Me,

_____

_____

_____

_____

_____

_____

_____

_____

_____

_____

_____

_____

_____

_____

_____

_____

Love, Future Me

LEARNING TO TRUST YOUR GUT:
CUTTING OUT THE OPINIONS THAT DON'T MATTER

As you take action to write your best story, you are going to face voices of distraction and opposition trying to discourage you, shame you, and even send you on a detour from living out your purpose. While you work on building trust in yourself through keeping promises, quieting your inner critic with self-love, and stepping into the unknown, you will find a confidence within you to endure these antagonistic characters. You may even feel empathy for them. (Remember: Critical people are very critical toward themselves too!) And anyway, what is a good story without obstacles, curveballs, and conflict? This is a part of being the main character. Take it as a compliment that you're so compelling. Your story is about to get good!

Picture this: You have a drum and you've been coming up with a beat on it, then you're thrown into a room with fifteen other people all playing their different beats. Now, you may be tempted to compare or change your beat. Your beat may begin to slowly change and morph into something else without you realizing it. If you don't spend time listening to what is deep inside of you, you will always be drawn to everyone else's noise. You may hear their beat, and lose your own. It will be difficult to fully develop your own distinguished sound. So how will you tune in so deeply to your own rhythm that the rhythms of others will fade away?

Exercise:

Identify activities that help you practice staying focused even when you have an audience or other distractions. Maybe meditation works well for you, or journaling? Maybe it's specific boundaries or habits, like not checking your phone first thing in the morning. What tools can you use to keep your focus? Brainstorm them here.

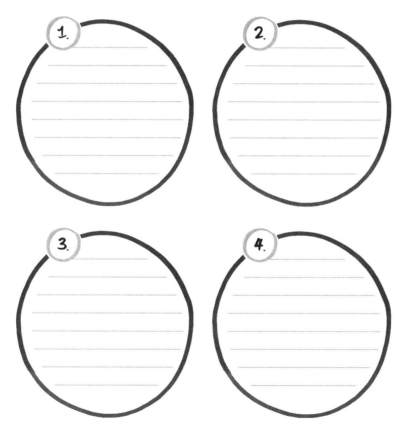

CHAPTER 16

What Is My Reward System?

Why do you want to be the main character, paving your unique path, writing your own story? Why do you want to do things differently than you have before? And why do you want to achieve your dreams? Because of the way it will make you feel. You want to feel a different way than you've felt before. You want to experience a new version of yourself—a happier, more content you. That is what has brought you to this point in this book (and in your life!). You want to feel a kind of fulfillment you haven't experienced. You want the joy of discovering your potential.

So how can you get that feeling without focusing on external validation? How can you avoid putting your own future and your own happiness into someone else's hands? By learning how to celebrate your effort, by positively looking at your "failures," and by being honest with yourself about what feeling you are searching for. You may have been on a quest for an external result—a visible achievement. But underneath that, you've been seeking an internal feeling, a state of *being*. Let's focus on that desired feeling and giving yourself the internal rewards you need to keep motivated in showing up the best way you can.

DEFINING SUCCESS:
HOW DO MY VALUES INFORM MY IDEA OF SUCCESS?

Everyone wants success. But what *is* success? It's not an objective, one-size-fits-all thing. Success for one person is different than success for another. But no matter what it looks like, success really comes down to achieving a desired feeling in the pursuit of your personal values. Money and cars and mansions and status are only the external results; what matters more are the values that are driving you.

You explored the things you value in the first quest of this book. What did you find out? Consider what has influenced you: What experience or person has taught you to value these things? Maybe you value humor because you felt loved and seen when people would give you positive attention for being funny. Or you value self-expression, because you have had a unique experience and desire to feel understood. Or you value your health because you've navigated health issues in the past and you want to feel freedom after those very limiting experiences. Some other values could include family, influence, adventure, faith, generosity, learning, friendship, and commitment. By practicing your values, you can find those great feelings you desire at each step of the journey—feelings like being loved, seen, heard, valued, appreciated, remembered, and more.

Exercise:

Identify three values that compel you. Connect the feeling(s) you hope to acquire in exercising these values in your life.

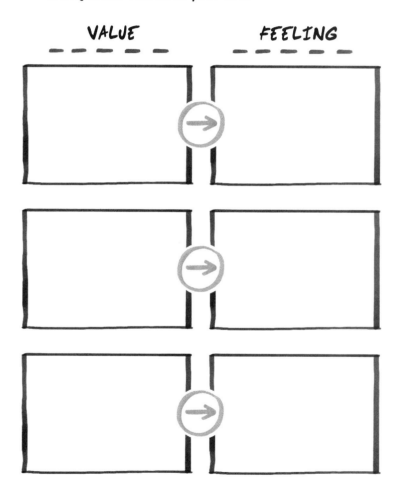

VALUE   FEELING

CELEBRATING YOUR INTERNAL GROWTH:
THERE'S VALUE IN THE JOURNEY

Why are we so destination-minded? "When I get there, *then* I'll be…" (Fill in the blank with *happy, loved, seen,* etc.) True, this kind of thinking can keep us motivated to take action. But is the outcome the only place where you can find what you are looking for? Or feel content? What if you could find that feeling in the journey? You are growing and becoming, learning and discovering every step of the way. Even if you feel stuck in a job you hate, you are gaining tools that prepare you to do better at a job you enjoy. Can you see yourself for all the effort you are putting in? Can you celebrate yourself right now for even showing up? Maybe you don't have to get somewhere specific to feel like you are successful and to be proud of yourself!

What makes this adventure rewarding is the self-discovery. Each step is enlightening you in a new way—if you fully embrace it. So instead of waiting to be in a literal spotlight where others can celebrate you, what if you could create your own spotlight and celebrate yourself? Many chapters of your story may not have visible growth or achievement. Those will be chapters where your roots are digging deep, so that you will be grounded when it is your time to shine. Can you find the hidden treasures that exist right here in this very chapter you are in?

Identify the areas of hidden growth that are happening in your life right now.

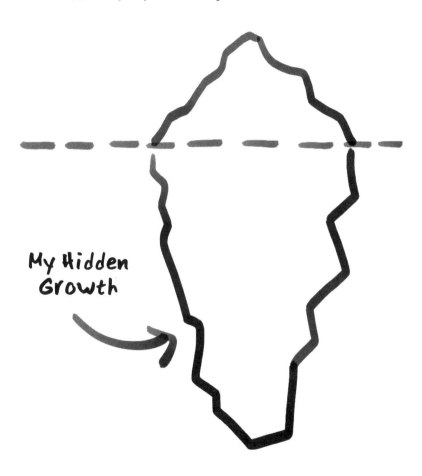

My Hidden Growth

CELEBRATING YOUR EFFORTS:
LOSSES ARE THE NEW WINS

In the previous exercise, you identified places where growth is already happening in your life. When you start to put more attention on the unseen part of the iceberg—the foundation hidden under the surface—you will begin to view challenges, obstacles, and losses in a new way. Instead of feeling downright unlucky or like you messed up, you can see that there is a valuable lesson where there is a loss. Each difficulty is a doorway inviting you to see yourself better and grow through meeting your challenges.

Where do you need to grow? What do you need to work on? Will you let the obstacles knock you off your feet, or will you see them as positive redirections? If it were all a test, would *you* level up? When you focus on your internal growth, when you can look for possibility in the midst of problems and find it within you to say "thank you" even when it seems like everything is crumbling…that's when you have found your resilience. And your resilience is a more valuable commodity than any singular opportunity. The external framework may fall apart, but no one can ever take away the internal framework of grit you have thoughtfully crafted inside of you.

Exercise:

Identify obstacles and challenges you have faced so far on your journey. How did you respond to them? What did you learn? Seeing your areas of vulnerability, how can you show up more prepared to face the obstacles ahead of you on your journey? Explore these questions here.

QUEST 3 REVIEW

In order to stay true to my "why" that I identified in the first quest, I will say no to anything that does not align with it. I will say no to:

_____
_____
_____
_____

To behave more like the person I want to become, three habits I need to break and three habits I need to make are:

_____
_____
_____
_____

What will I focus on that is within my control?

_____

Because I know it's not too late for me to start something new, what will I try?

_____

Because I am competing against myself, and my own growth, what will I faithfully work toward getting better at?

_____

Why do I value my internal growth?

_____

INDEX

ABOUT THE AUTHOR

Crystal St. John is an actress, writer, and singer residing in Los Angeles with her filmmaker husband. A motivational content creator on TikTok, Crystal has always had a deep passion for nontraditional teaching through storytelling. Growing up, she struggled with feeling like she wasn't enough or she didn't belong, which left her with a limited mindset and a fearful heart, and set her on a quest to chase a courageous life—one where she would be the main character.